JEHOVAH'S WITNESSES
ON TRIAL

JEHOVAH'S WITNESSES ON TRIAL

THE TESTIMONY OF THE EARLY CHURCH FATHERS

ROBERT U. FINNERTY

PUBLISHING
P.O. BOX 817 • PHILLIPSBURG • NEW JERSEY 08865

Unless otherwise indicated, Scripture quotations are from the HOLY BIBLE, NEW INTERNATIONAL VERSION. Copyright © 1973, 1978, 1984 International Bible Society. Used by permission of Zondervan Bible Publishers.

Manufactured in the United States of America

Library of Congress Cataloging-in-Publication Data

Finnerty, Robert U., 1950-
    Jehovah's Witnesses on trial : the testimony of the early church fathers / Robert U. Finnerty.
        p.   cm.
    Includes bibliographical references and index.
    ISBN 0-87552-240-8
    1. Watch Tower Bible and Tract Society—Controversial literature. 2. Jehovah's Witnesses—Controversial literature. 3. Fathers of the church. I. Title.
BX8526.5.F56   1993
289.9'2—dc20   92-42682

To

CYNTHIA—
whose steadfast love has made this all possible;

BILL, KATE, AND MARY—
that you may embrace the faith of our dearest Lord and Savior
Jesus Christ, and be transformed by his love;

GREG PASTOR—
whose lively discussions started my journey down this road;

and

HERB, SCOTTY, AND GEORGE,
and my many other Witness friends on Compuserve—
that you may come to know him who is life,
and that he might set you free.

Contents

Foreword

During the past two decades many excellent books have been published by critics of the Jehovah's Witnesses. These have covered new, never before treated subjects, have been the personal accounts of ex-Witnesses, or have updated and expanded on what was previously written. *Jehovah's Witnesses on Trial* provides a brief and helpful survey of Witness history and doctrines; however, the focus of the study is an examination of the early church fathers and the Witnesses' use of them. In recent years this subject has become an important one because Watchtower publications have increasingly made reference to the Fathers in support of their theology or in refutation of orthodoxy.

Robert Finnerty demonstrates a thorough knowledge of Witness publications and the sources pertinent to his examination of the patristic literature. Several times in his study he challenges and encourages the reader to examine personally the primary sources that he presents, and he makes this as convenient as possible by full documentation in the reference notes at the end of each chapter. This approach is contrary to what one often finds in Watchtower publications such as the booklet *Should You Believe in the Trinity?* (1989), where page numbers and other revelant information for the sources cited are not included in the text.

Finnerty's careful examination of the church fathers in the primary sources shows that the Witnesses have misrepresented them. He finds that the scholarship in the Witness materials examined is shallow or even dishonest. He concludes not only that Witness theology receives no support from the writings of the Fathers, but instead, when correctly understood, these writings offer a refutation of their teachings. The real roots of the theology of the Jehovah's Witnesses are to be found in the nineteenth-century teachings of C. T. Russell and in the older heretical teachings of deviations from Christianity.

This is an important book for those who are concerned with historical and biblical truth and with the exposure of Witness deception. This study should have a wide circulation. It is with great pleasure that I recommend this book as a helpful and needed tool.

Finally, Finnerty is interested not only in the communication of truth to those who may be deceived; he is just as concerned for their salvation. May all who know the Savior and who use this book in their outreach to Jehovah's Witnesses follow the instruction and spirit of Paul in 2 Timothy 2:24-26.

And the Lord's servant must not quarrel; instead, he must be kind to everyone, able to teach, not resentful. Those who oppose him he must gently instruct, in the hope that God will grant them repentance leading them to a knowledge of the truth, and that they will come to their senses and escape from the trap of the devil, who has taken them captive to do his will.

EDMOND C. GRUSS

1

The Fathers and the Witnesses

The church has always had rivals. Before the dust had settled on the Roman roads walked by the apostles, alternative theologies were springing up and challenging apostolic doctrine. Some proposed a Jesus who was merely a man filled with the Spirit of God, the Messiah by virtue of his keeping the law perfectly. Others followed the call to a higher knowledge than the apostolic gospel seemed to provide, a knowledge given only to the few. From the first, the church of Christ and his apostles were destined to battle the insidious onslaught of seductive half-truths and reasonable falsehoods.

The apostolic church was not without weapons, however. Foremost was the powerful testimony of eyewitnesses to Christ's life and resurrection, which was preserved first as verifiable oral tradition and later as the written Word. The writings of the apostles and their disciples, which formed the New Testament canon, served well in the defense of the faith and indeed became its very cornerstone.

In the first few centuries after the death of the apostles, as the church grew and matured, the literary efforts of other men, held in high esteem as leaders and teachers of the church, also served to communicate and defend the faith. These writings were highly regarded and sometimes were circulated in conjunction with the Scriptures themselves. They became in time an integral part of the spiritual literature of the growing Christian communities and were frequently included in the liturgy. These works were carefully preserved by the church, and copies of many of them have survived to modern times. The authors, generally referred to as the apostolic or church fathers, have provided through their literary efforts an invaluable resource for understanding the history and development of Christian life, beliefs, and doctrine in the postapostolic age.

The discourses of the Fathers were prompted by circumstances both internal and external to the life of the church. Some compositions, such as the apologies of Justin Martyr, were written to explain and defend Christianity to pagan authorities in an attempt to deflect persecution. Others, much like the letters of the apostle Paul, were written to encourage, teach, and correct wayward churches. Many were written to defend the church against heresies arising from inside and outside the Christian community.

The writings of the Fathers have proved to be of great value in many areas of Christian doctrine and historical tradition. The authors frequently and extensively quote

Scripture, thereby providing evidence to Bible translators of early manuscripts no longer extant. Valuable and fascinating insights may be gained into the structure and authority of the early church, detailed by those who steadfastly followed in the footsteps of apostolic authority. Particularly pertinent to the contemporary church, which is under assault from every side for its traditional beliefs, is the insight these writings furnish into the formation of orthodox Christian doctrine, particularly as it developed in response to heresy.

Contemporary Christians often have little appreciation of the lengthy process by which orthodox doctrine developed. There is a tendency to understand this process in a simplistic fashion—the early church, the thinking goes, simply "believed what's taught in the Scriptures." For several centuries, however, the exact content of the Scriptures, which we call "the canon," was disputed to some degree. In the very earliest years of the church, apostolic teaching was largely transmitted by oral tradition. The importance of such transmission is evident in many writings of the early church, where tremendous emphasis is laid on accurate, detailed accounting of the testimony of those who were eyewitnesses to New Testament events and apostolic teaching.

Since the Reformation, the Protestant church has tended to minimize the importance of tradition (and hence the sources for this tradition) in Christian doctrine, largely in reaction to perceived abuses by the medieval church. Luther emphasized *sola Scriptura* ("Scripture alone") in response to what he understood as departures from New Testament faith and biblical teaching. With that emphasis, however, came a diminished appreciation of both the church fathers and the great creedal statements of the fourth and fifth centuries. Partly as a result of this trend, there arose an age of individualistic interpretation of Scripture, resulting in such aberrations as liberalism and humanism, which continue to plague the church today. Harold Brown, in his study of the history of heresy in the church, expresses this problem well when he says:

> The Reformation claims as its reason for existence that it is far more faithful to the biblical message and historic Christianity than traditional Roman Catholicism. . . . Nevertheless, the Reformation quickly produced far more doctrinal chaos than the Church had experienced since the second century, when it had to contend with Gnosticism, Marcionism, and Montanism all at the same time.[1]

Included in the heritage of doctrinal chaos in the post-Reformation era are sects such as the Latter-day Saints (Mormons) and the Jehovah's Witnesses. These groups have used a highly individualistic approach to interpreting the Bible in order to justify many of their doctrines. By this process they have promoted heresies that must be dealt with by the modern church.

Study of the history and development of Christian doctrine reveals that many orthodox doctrines, such as the Trinity and the two natures of Christ, were refined over an extended period, primarily in response to heresy. This is not to say that these beliefs were foreign to the teachings of Christ and the apostles. In a very real sense, however, they were often only implicitly understood by the church at its outset. The first-century church, besieged as it was by persecution, and expecting the imminent return of Christ, spent no time developing detailed doctrinal positions or writing theological treatises, as such efforts were little needed. It was not until the threat of numerous heresies arose that Christian scholars undertook the formidable task of precisely elucidating the "faith that was once for all entrusted to the saints" (Jude 3). The writings of the church fathers give us a glimpse of the history and development of these doctrines, and they show us how the shepherds and defenders of the early church understood the apostolic faith. Furthermore, their vigorous refutation of heresy manifests the heart of the Christian faith.

The cults that plague and challenge Christianity today frequently resemble the heretical groups encountered by the early church. They deny in particular those tenets of the Christian faith which were honed and developed in reaction to heretical thought, such as the Trinity. In this regard, the writings of the church fathers are valuable resources for the modern church in defending the faith against the cults. The cults frequently claim to represent the "true church," restored after centuries of apostasy by "Christendom." The testimony of the Fathers, bearing witness as it does to the true faith of all believers in the Lord Jesus Christ, is a powerful resource for refuting such claims. The writings of these early Christians can therefore be used effectively to sow seeds of doubt in the minds of cult members about the claims of their organizations.

The Jehovah's Witnesses (the Watchtower Society) have been selected for comparison with the apostolic fathers because, of all sects, they alone claim to base their beliefs exclusively on the Bible, maintaining along with orthodox Christianity the inspiration and inerrancy of the Scriptures. Yet in spite of their ostensibly biblical foundation, the Witnesses arrive at radically different doctrines.

To justify their wide departure from the traditional Christian faith, the Witness literature has increasingly drawn upon documents from the first few centuries after the apostles for support. Although the Watchtower Society was not organized until the latter part of the nineteenth century, the Witnesses maintain that their teachings alone are faithful to those of the apostles and the early church. They assert that "Christendom" (i.e., organized Christianity, both Catholic and Protestant) is the "apostasy foretold by Jesus."[2] As a result of pagan influences, they say, the nominal Christian church lost the true faith by the latter part of the second century. This process supposedly culminated in the establishment of heretical doctrines, such as those of the Trinity, the immortality of the soul, and eternal punishment, which were subsequently formalized in the Nicene and other creeds produced by church councils. Recent Watchtower literature has begun to utilize directly the writings of the ante-Nicene fathers to substantiate their doctrinal positions, thereby undermining the tradition supporting orthodox belief.[3] An examination of the early church writings themselves, therefore, would certainly be most appropriate in order to evaluate the Witnesses' positions.

The writings of the apostolic fathers, rather than the Scriptures themselves, have been selected to counter the doctrines of the Jehovah's Witnesses for several reasons. First of all, there is no shortage of excellent expository and apologetic writing on the teachings of the Watchtower Society. Walter Martin[4], Edmond Gruss[5], and numerous others[6] have exposed the many discrepancies and errors of the Society's doctrines, judged by the light of careful, thorough biblical exposition. Little is to be gained by repeating their work.

Secondly, the Bible, which can be a challenge to understand, is easily misinterpreted by those who rend its parts out of context to "prove" their doctrinal presuppositions. This approach has been raised to a fine art by the followers of Charles Russell. The writings of the apostolic fathers are less susceptible to such misinterpretation. The Fathers often state quite plainly those things upon which the Scriptures (particularly individual verses taken out of context) seem at times to equivocate. For example, there are relatively few explicit references in the New Testament to the deity of Christ (although unbiased biblical exposition demonstrates his deity decisively). The Witnesses have developed elaborate ways to get around these verses, and they have even changed their translation in some instances to support their theology. This can present a significant hurdle to overcome in evangelism. The church fathers, on the other hand, make it clear that the deity of Christ was at the heart of the Christian faith, and their writings are more difficult to twist in support of erroneous theological formulations. Furthermore, the early fathers were often writing for the express purpose of refuting heretical theology—theology that modern sects such as the Witnesses often reflect. Hence, many of their statements are stinging rebuttals to speculative theological viewpoints propounded by the Watchtower Society and others.

Lastly, those who are involved in evangelism to Jehovah's Witnesses often find them remarkably immune to scriptural exposition, no matter how thorough and well documented. Jehovah's Witnesses will generally reject anything contrary to what they have accepted as "meat in due season"—the interpretations presented in the Watchtower Society's literature. The writings of the church fathers can provide additional grounds on which the teachings of the Watchtower Society may be questioned in an evangelistic context.

The Christian church, under the guidance of the Holy Spirit, spent several centuries clearly defining and carefully delineating what is unquestionably its most controversial tenet to nonbelievers: the doctrine of the Trinity. This should not be surprising in light of the profundity of the event described by John, "The Word became flesh, and dwelt among us" (John 1:14, NASB). The revelation of God as three distinct persons, coequal and coeternal, while present in fact, is largely implicit both in the Scriptures and in the faith of the apostolic church. As a result, the church appears vulnerable on this dogma. Indeed, it has undergone relentless attack from the first because of its belief in the triune God. The Jehovah's Witnesses are eager participants in this onslaught, and they delight in attacking this most hated doctrine of apostate Christendom. It is tremendously beneficial to the defense of this truth to demonstrate, as can be done with little difficulty, that the essential components of the doctrine of the Trinity are present in the writings of those who were disciples of the apostles.

The church fathers were in no way a homogeneous group. Counted in their ranks were pastors and poets, philosophers and martyrs, lawyers and bishops. They wrote in styles that ranged from elegant prose to tedious allegory. Their works do not have the spiritual power or literary impact of the New Testament. Yet radiating from their writings is a faith passed down from the apostles and a passion for their Lord who had died and risen for them. It is in their light that any who now claim to be the repository of Christian truth must stand for examination.

NOTES

1. Harold O. Brown, *Heresies* (Grand Rapids: Baker, 1984), 341.
2. *The Divine Name That Will Endure Forever* (Brooklyn: Watchtower Bible and Tract Society of Pennsylvania, 1984), 25.
3. *Should You Believe in the Trinity?* (Brooklyn: Watchtower Bible and Tract Society of Pennsylvania, 1989), 7; *Watchtower,* October 1, 1989, 6; ibid., July 15, 1990, 21–23.
4. Walter R. Martin and Norman H. Klann, *Jehovah of the Watchtower* (Minneapolis: Bethany House, 1974).
5. Edmond C. Gruss, *Apostles of Denial* (Phillipsburg, N.J.: Presbyterian and Reformed, 1970).
6. See for example Robert M. Bowman, Jr., *Why You Should Believe in the Trinity: An Answer to Jehovah's Witnesses* (Grand Rapids: Baker, 1989). By focusing on the Trinitarian question, Bowman offers fuller discussion of a number of points made independently here.

2

The History and Major Doctrines of the Jehovah's Witnesses

HISTORY

The Jehovah's Witnesses movement was begun by Charles Taze Russell. He was born in Old Allegheny, Pennsylvania, on February 16, 1852, to Joseph and Eliza Birney Russell, both of Scotch-Irish lineage. Reared in an orthodox Congregational church, he worked in his early adult years in his father's clothing store. At the age of seventeen, apparently as a result of his failure to convert an unbelieving friend to Christianity, Russell himself became a skeptic. The issue that seems to have been decisive in this transformation was the doctrine of eternal punishment. Russell concluded, "A God that would use his power to create human beings whom he foreknew and predestinated should be eternally tormented, could be neither wise, just nor loving. His standard would be lower than that of many men."[1] So he rejected this doctrine and began to reexamine the Bible, using reason as his principal guide. Several years later he encountered the Adventists, who further strengthened his beliefs about hell and fostered in him an interest in biblical chronology and the second coming of Christ. He eventually developed differences with the Adventists and broke with them, forming his own Bible study group, which later appointed him "Pastor."[2]

Russell approached the Scriptures with the idea that their interpretation must be subject to human reason. Using this process, he developed his "Present Truth" theology, which was characterized by a rejection of virtually every major Christian doctrine as "unreasonable and unscriptural" and was punctuated by a strong aversion to organized religion and government. His movement gained numerous converts, owing in no small part to Russell's astute business and promotional sense and his widely distributed publications. In 1884 he established the Watchtower Society as a vehicle for the publication of his writings. His literary accomplishments included thirteen books, countless newspaper articles recounting his "sermons" (few of which were actually delivered), and the monthly periodical *Zion's Watch Tower*, which later became the *Watchtower*. These writings presented Russell's studies in the Scriptures, in which chronology and prophetic interpretation were prominently featured. These literary efforts convinced his followers that he was God's spokesman on earth, on a par with the apostle Paul and Martin Luther.[3] Russell was widely regarded by his admirers as the "faithful and wise servant" of Matthew 24:48—God's channel of revelation to his people.[4]

On October 31, 1916, after a brief illness, Russell died while on a train en route to a speaking tour, dressed in a Roman toga.[5] He was succeeded in leadership by Joseph F. "Judge" Rutherford.[6] Born in Missouri in 1869, Rutherford had some formal education, unlike his predecessor. He was a practicing lawyer (although he never received a formal law degree) when he encountered Russellism in 1894. By 1907 he was deeply involved in the Watchtower Society and had become its legal counsel. After a brief power struggle, he was elected president of the Society in January 1917. Like Russell, Rutherford vigorously pursued reason-based Scripture studies, further developing and modifying the doctrines of Russellism. His most significant challenge was to transfer the loyalty of Society members from Russell, who was regarded by his followers as a prophet and spokesman for God, to the organization, the Watchtower Society, of which Rutherford was the unrivaled leader. After several years of consolidating his position, which drove out many Bible Students (as Russell's followers were known), Rutherford had established an organization in which unquestioning obedience was the rule.[7] The "faithful and wise servant" was now very definitely the organization rather than Russell, providing "meat in due season" to its unquestioning followers.[8]

After serving a short prison term in 1918 for publishing antiwar literature (an internment that served him well by fostering his image as a religious martyr), Rutherford became even more vehement than his mentor in his attacks on government and organized religion. He shifted the Society's doctrinal emphasis from the atonement and the restitution of all things, which had been key concepts under Russell, to the vindication of Jehovah's name. The doctrinal changes and the rejection of Russell's personality cult were ultimately crystallized in 1931, when the Society changed its name to the Jehovah's Witnesses. Rutherford's literary output and oratorical skills dwarfed those of his predecessor and did much to encourage the vigorous growth of the organization during his years of tenure.

Rutherford died in January 1942 at the Beth Sarim mansion, a house the Society had built to accommodate Abraham, Isaac, and Jacob, who had failed to show up for their resurrection as prophesied to take place in 1925.[9] He was succeeded by Nathan Knorr. Born in Bethlehem, Pennsylvania, in 1905, Knorr first associated with the Bible Students at age 16. As the Society's president, he oversaw a vigorous program of expansion. His leadership, although not nearly as charismatic as that of his mentors, nevertheless resulted in rapid growth for the organization, which increased in membership from 115,000 at his election to over 2,000,000 by 1975. It was during his tenure and under his supervision that the Society's version of the Bible, the *New World Translation*, was completed in 1950. Although Knorr lacked the doctrinal creativity of his predecessors, his strong emphasis on education and training programs fostered an era of tremendous growth. As a result of his efforts, Jehovah's Witnesses became substantially better equipped to argue their theology with others and win converts. Nathan Knorr died of brain cancer in June 1977.

Knorr was succeeded by Fred W. Franz, the Society's principal resource for writing and scriptural interpretation during Knorr's tenure. Generally considered one of the Society's best scholars, he studied Greek for two years at the University of Cincinnati. But he dropped out in 1914 because of the global turmoil then predicted.[10] Franz assumed the vice-presidency in 1944 and was elected president following Knorr's death in 1977, a position he still holds today. The nature of the Society's presidency changed radically shortly after his election, however. In January 1976, after a period of considerable turmoil within the organization, its power structure was markedly altered. The Governing Body, a committee of approximately seventeen members, assumed power and became responsible for all teachings and decisions of the Society. Since the inception of the Society, the Governing Body had been little more than a rubber-stamp committee for the all-powerful president. As a result of this transition, however, the Governing Body assumed the same dictatorial power over the flock that Russell and Rutherford had once held, and the power of the presidency was much diluted. Franz has remained the organization's most revered scholar, however.[11]

MAJOR DOCTRINES

The beliefs of the Jehovah's Witnesses, in keeping with their confidence in "progressive revelation" through the God-ordained channel of the Watchtower Society, have undergone considerable change over the years, a process readily discerned by a historical review of their literature.[12] Nevertheless, their major doctrines have remained fairly

15

stable since they were first put forth by Russell over a century ago. The following summary of their major doctrinal positions is based upon the Society's own literature. Subsequent chapters will provide more detailed analysis of the Witnesses' teachings.

THE BIBLE

Jehovah's Witnesses believe that the Bible is God's inspired Word and the authoritative source for all doctrine and belief. The Watchtower Society alone, however, has the key to understanding God's Word.

> Thus the Bible is an organizational book and belongs to the Christian congregation as an organization, not to individuals, regardless of how sincerely they may believe that they can interpret the Bible.[13]

> The world is full of Bibles, which book contains the commandments of God. Why, then, do the people not know which way to go? Because they do not also have the teaching or law of the mother, which is light. . . . If we are to walk in the truth we must recognize not only Jehovah God as our father but his organization as our mother.[14]

GOD

There is only one almighty God, whose name is Jehovah. All of human history is focused on the vindication of Jehovah's name, which was defiled by Satan's rebellion and man's subsequent fall.

In time these faithful servants of Jehovah came to realize that the vindication of Jehovah's name is the great issue confronting mankind, and that this is far more important, even, than the salvation of human creatures.[15]

JESUS CHRIST

Jesus is the first and greatest of God's created beings. He was known as Michael the Archangel in his prehuman state and was Jehovah's chief agent in the creation process. While on earth, he was a perfect human being, nothing more. Jesus died on the cross as a ransom for the sin of Adam alone, to allow man a second chance to serve Jehovah. He was raised by Jehovah, not in the flesh, but as a spirit creature. After his ascension to heaven, he was exalted because of his obedience, and he will return to execute judgment on all those who reject Jehovah's plan of salvation.

THE HOLY SPIRIT

The "holy spirit" (never capitalized) is not God, or a person, but rather an impersonal force that executes Jehovah's will.

THE TRINITY

The doctrine of the Trinity is pagan in origin and instituted by Satan. It was introduced in the second century as a result of the apostasy of the nominal Christian church ("Christendom"), and it was solidified as false doctrine at Nicaea and subsequent church councils.

THE SOUL

Man does not possess an immortal soul, but rather is himself a "soul." The soul of man talked about in the Scriptures is his breath, and it represents the combination of his flesh and his spirit or "life force." It is no different from the soul of animals. The spirit or life force is not personal, but rather an impersonal force, like electricity. At death, man ceases to exist. The doctrine of the immortality of the soul is of pagan origin.

ETERNAL PUNISHMENT

Jehovah's Witnesses strongly deny the doctrine of eternal punishment, in keeping with the convictions of their founder, Charles Russell. There is no conscious eternal punishment for wickedness. Death is the final punishment for the wicked; the just alone will be raised to eternal life in the resurrection.

THE RESURRECTION

The resurrection is not the restoration of an individual by joining his soul to a resurrection body; it is the re-creation of the individual from the life pattern contained in the memory of God. The Witnesses believe in three resurrections:

The First Resurrection. This is a spiritual resurrection and applies only to Christ and 144,000 select followers. None of the 144,000 was raised until 1918, after the second, invisible *parousia* (coming) of Christ in 1914. In this resurrection the affected individuals receive spirit bodies, invisible to the human eye.

The Resurrection to Life. This is an earthly resurrection, in which the dead are raised to physical bodies. Included in this resurrection are (1) those faithful witnesses who died before the time of Christ (i.e., the Old Testament prophets and saints) and (2) the "other sheep"—faithful Jehovah's Witnesses who will have died before Armageddon. This resurrection will occur early during the millennium, the thousand-year reign of Christ. The wicked who have sinned against the holy spirit will not be raised.

The Resurrection of Judgment. The last resurrection, which occurs after Armageddon, includes well-intentioned men who have not heard the gospel of the kingdom.

SALVATION

In Watchtower doctrine, this is understood from the perspective of two classes, the "Congregation of God" (also known as the "anointed class," the "Remnant," or the "144,000") and the "Great Crowd." The Congregation of God hopes to dwell with Christ in heaven, if they remain faithful to his organization. This class is restricted to 144,000 individuals who alone are "spirit begotten" (born again). Dwelling in an earthly paradise, not in heaven, is the hope of the Great Crowd. This class is composed of the vast majority of Jehovah's Witnesses. Salvation for the Great Crowd is not by faith alone, although faith in Jehovah God and his Son Jesus Christ is nominally required. Salvation is fundamentally obtained by works. The Society lists four requirements for salvation: (1) knowledge—"knowledge of God's purposes . . . by studying the Bible"; (2) obedience—"obey God's laws"; (3) association with the channel—"be associated with God's channel, his organization. . . . To receive everlasting life in the earthly Paradise we must identify that organization and serve God as part of it"; and (4) witnessing—"God requires that prospective subjects of His kingdom support His government by loyally advocating His Kingdom rule to others."[16]

GOVERNMENT

All human governments are under the influence of Satan and have usurped the authority of Jehovah to rule over man. All religions are likewise under Satan's command, particularly the churches of apostate Christendom. All human governments and the apostate churches (together known as "Babylon") will be destroyed in the great Battle of Armageddon, after which Jehovah will establish his theocratic rule on earth. Armageddon is imminent; the generation that saw the signs of Christ's return in 1914 will see the ushering in of his earthly kingdom.

THE SECOND COMING

Although Russell taught that Christ returned invisibly in 1874 and predicted that Armageddon would be completed by 1914,[17] current Watchtower doctrine is that Christ returned invisibly in 1914. The Day of Wrath has been predicted at various years subsequent to this. The *parousia* ("coming," or as the Witnesses prefer to translate it, "presence") of Christ in either scenario is perceived only by his faithful followers. The year 1914 is arrived at by complex computations based on the supposed fall of Jerusalem in 607 B.C. (the consensus of historians is that it occurred in 587 B.C.) and the prophecy of "seven times" in

Daniel 4. The year 1914 marks the beginning of the "time of the end" of Bible prophecy. Three and a half years later, in 1918, Christ's true followers who had died, from the apostles onward, were resurrected to reign in heaven. About the same time, Christ anointed his living followers to function as his "faithful and discreet slave," his approved agency for his work on earth. The "slave" would serve as his sole channel for communicating guidance and illumination to his servants worldwide. The generation that was alive and able to comprehend the signs of the times in 1914 is "the generation that will not pass away until all things are fulfilled."[18]

These, briefly, are the major doctrines of the Watchtower Society. Each of them is said to be solely biblical in origin. Moreover, Jehovah's Witnesses claim to be in complete harmony with the teachings of the apostolic church and early Christians, at least until the time of the "great apostasy." In recent years, and with increasing frequency, the Society has been affirming the authenticity of its doctrines by utilizing the works of the early church fathers. The validity of these claims is the focus of the following chapters.

NOTES

1. Charles T. Russell, *The Divine Plan of the Ages* (Brooklyn: International Bible Students Association, 1924), Biography supp., 1.
2. Edmond C. Gruss, *Apostles of Denial* (Phillipsburg, N.J.: Presbyterian and Reformed, 1970), 38–39.
3. *The Finished Mystery* (Brooklyn: International Bible Students Association, 1917), 367.

4. Duane Magnani, *Who Is the Faithful and Wise Servant?* (Clayton, Calif.: Witness Inc., 1979), 169–72.
5. Russell, *Divine Plan of the Ages*, 20–21.
6. While serving as a legal clerk in a Missouri court, Rutherford spent four days as acting judge in the presiding judge's absence, a practice not uncommon at the time. From this brief but illustrious career he acquired the title "Judge."
7. William J. Schnell *Thirty Years a Watchtower Slave* (Grand Rapids: Baker, 1971), 40–62.
8. Gruss, *Apostles of Denial*, 53–55, 61.
9. *Millions Now Living Will Never Die* (Brooklyn: International Bible Students Association, 1920), 68, 89.
10. Proceedings—*Douglas Walsh vs. WTBTS* (Scotland, 1954), 91.
11. Raymond Franz, *Crisis of Conscience* (Atlanta: Commentary Press, 1983), 67–94 .
12. The Society's older literature is very difficult to obtain. Several organizations (most notably Witness, Inc., P. O. Box 597, Clayton, CA 94517) have extensively researched the Society's publications and have photocopies of this material available.
13. *Watchtower*, Oct. 1, 1967, 587.
14. Ibid., May 1, 1957, 274.
15. Ibid., Dec. 1, 1981, 24.
16. Ibid., 252.
17. Charles T. Russell, *Studies in the Scriptures*, vol. 2: *The Time Is at Hand* (Brooklyn: International Bible Students Association, 1889), 101.
18. Franz, *Crisis of Conscience*, 139.

3

The Deity and Nature of Jesus Christ

Who is this wonderful God? Some persons say his name is Jesus. Others say he is a Trinity, although the word "trinity" does not appear in the Bible. . . . Well, did Jesus ever say that he was God? No, he never did. . . . He said, "The Father is greater than I am." . . . Jesus explained that there were things that neither he nor the angels knew but that only God knew. . . . On one occasion Jesus prayed to God, saying: "Let, not my will, but yours take place." If Jesus were Almighty God, he would not have prayed

to himself, would he? . . . Thus the Almighty God
and Jesus are clearly two separate persons. Even after his death and resurrection and ascension to
heaven, Jesus was still not equal to his Father.[1]

Thus begins the section on Jesus in *You Can Live Forever in Paradise on Earth*, the basic instruction manual for
those studying to become Jehovah's Witnesses. Although
the deity of Christ is the central belief of orthodox Christianity, it has been a stumbling block for many down
through the centuries. As Martin and Klann say, "The deity of Jesus Christ is one of the cornerstones of Christianity, and as such has been attacked more vigorously throughout the ages than any other single doctrine of the Christian
faith."[2] Jehovah's Witnesses, while claiming to be Christian, oppose this fundamental doctrine. In so doing, they
join a long line of spiritual ancestors who have rejected Jesus' claim to be God in the flesh (John 8:58). Basically, they
follow the teachings of Arius, a fourth-century heretic.[3]

The Watchtower Society has shown considerable doctrinal flexibility over the years on many issues, but it has
always been unwavering in its opposition to the deity of
Christ. In his *Studies in the Scriptures*, Charles Russell propounded this Arian doctrine.

Our Redeemer existed as a spirit being before he
was made flesh and dwelt amongst men. At that
time, as well as subsequently, he was properly
known as "a god"—a mighty one.[4]

The Logos himself was "the beginning of the creation of God. . . . The Logos was himself the only
direct creation or begetting of the Heavenly Father."[5]

24

The present view of the Watchtower Society regarding Christ varies little if any from Russell's theology. It teaches that Jesus is an angel, the first and greatest creation of Jehovah God. He is known as the "only begotten" by virtue of his being the only living creature personally engendered by Jehovah. All other beings have been created by Jesus as Jehovah's agent. In heaven, prior to his human existence, Jesus was a "mighty spirit creature" known as Michael. When the time came for Jesus to become a man:

> Jehovah transferred the life of his mighty spirit Son from heaven to the womb of the virgin Mary. . . . So before being born on earth as a man Jesus had been in heaven as a mighty spirit person. He had a spirit body invisible to man, just as God has.[6]

On earth, however, Jesus was not an angelic being in human flesh, but only a man.

> By this miracle he was born a man. . . . He was not a spirit-human hybrid, a man and at the same time a spirit person. . . . He was flesh.[7]

> Because he was a perfect man, even as Adam had been, Jesus is called "the last Adam." . . . Jesus is the only man who ever lived that was equal to Adam as a perfect human son of God.[8]

The Witnesses' teaching varies widely from historic Christianity in other key areas of the life and work of Jesus Christ. The doctrine of Christ's ransom for the sin of his people and the truth of his bodily resurrection and visible bodily return, while presented in familiar language in the Society's publications, assume a meaning quite foreign to the traditional Christian faith. At times the Witnesses sound tantalizingly orthodox, as when they explain the importance of Christ's ransom for the sin of man.

> Even now Jesus' ransom sacrifice can benefit us. How? By exercising faith in it we can enjoy a clean standing before God and come under his loving and tender care. . . . We can freely seek forgiveness from God on the basis of the ransom, with confidence that he will hear us.[9]

Closer examination of Watchtower literature, however, reveals a teaching that is diametrically opposed to biblical and historic Christian doctrine of the atonement. For the Jehovah's Witness, the ransom of Jesus Christ does not pay the penalty for all of his sins—past, present, and future. The gospel preached by the Witnesses asserts that the death of Jesus pays only for the sin of Adam, purchasing for most men only the right to live in a paradise on earth.[10] However, one is also required to associate with God's organization and live a life of obedience to God's law, if one is to reap the benefits of the ransom.

> The ransom does not excuse sin in any. . . . It merely releases the accepting sinner from the first condemnation and its results . . . and places him again on trial for life, in which trial his own willful obedience or willful disobedience will decide whether he may or may not have life everlasting.[11]

> By his disobedience the perfect man Adam lost perfect life on a paradise earth for himself and all his

children. Jesus Christ gave his own perfect life to buy back what Adam lost.[12]

The Watchtower doctrine of the ransom rejects the sufficiency of Christ's sacrifice for man's individual sinfulness. It merely gives the Witness a new opportunity to prove himself by obedience and organizational affiliation.

The bodily resurrection of Jesus has shone as the beacon of hope for all who profess his name. It points to the time when his followers will be raised to resurrection life with him. This central doctrine of the Christian faith has been attacked from every quarter. This assault began with the Gnostic heresies of the first and second centuries. The Gnostics were dualists who considered the material world to be hopelessly estranged from the spiritual realm. They considered it unthinkable that a pure spiritual being, the Logos, would have suffered physical torture and death. Therefore, they set forth the doctrine, called docetism, that Christ had only seemed to be a man or to suffer in the flesh. The spiritual Logos departed prior to the Crucifixion, but manifested himself to the disciples after his "resurrection" as an incorruptible spirit being.[13] The Gnostic *Gospel of Truth*, discovered among the Nag Hammadi manuscripts in Egypt in 1947, puts it this way:

> He was nailed to a tree. . . . He humbled himself even to death although eternal life clothed him. After he had laid aside these perishable rags [his body] he clothed himself with incorruptibility which no one can take from him.[14]

The "incorruptibility" spoken of here is a common Gnostic concept. It refers to that which is pure spirit, in

27

contrast to the corrupt and unredeemable material world. The Gnostics conceived of Christ as the embodiment of the spirit Logos, who, at his death or just prior to it, put aside his hopelessly corrupted flesh. In his resurrection, he "clothed himself" with a pure spiritual body or essence.

Charles Russell and his followers adopted a doctrine of the Resurrection that resembles Gnosticism. They modified docetism to fit in with their doctrine of soul death.[15] They do not deny the physical suffering and death of Jesus, but they maintain that at the moment of his death he ceased to exist. Thus, there was no Son of God for the three days his body lay in the tomb. The Witnesses claim that God disposed of Jesus' body, as he had with that of Moses, and that Jesus "arose" on the third day as a glorified spirit creature.

> When Jesus Christ died, he . . . was unconscious, out of existence. Death did not mean a transition to another life for Jesus; rather, nonexistence.[16]

> The Bible is very clear when it says, "Christ died once for all time concerning sins . . . he being put to death in the flesh, but being made alive in the spirit." . . . Only spirit persons with spiritual bodies can live in heaven.[17]

The postresurrection appearances to the disciples (Luke 24:13-31), the insertion of Thomas's hand into the wounds of the risen Christ (John 20:27-28), and Jesus' statement to his disciples after the Resurrection, "Touch me and see; a ghost does not have flesh and bones, as you see I have" (Luke 24:39), present little difficulty to the Society, for they say:

28

Since the apostle Thomas was able to put his hand into a hole in Jesus' side, does that not show that Jesus was raised from the dead in the same body that was nailed to the stake? No, for Jesus simply materialized or took on a fleshly body, as angels had done in the past.[18]

The return of Christ, in Watchtower theology, is also quite different from orthodox Christian belief. Since Jesus was raised as an invisible spirit creature, his return would be neither physical nor visible to the unbeliever.

What was the manner of Jesus' leaving? . . . The departing Jesus, therefore, became invisible to [the disciples]. . . . Thus his return also would be invisible, in a spiritual body.[19]

Russell's doctrine of the return of Christ, which was officially held by the Society until the 1940s, maintained that Jesus returned invisibly in 1874, but was seen only by the faithful followers of the "Present Truth." The Society currently teaches that this event occurred in 1914—a change of dates unknown to most Witnesses. Watchtower theology also dispenses with another key aspect of Christ's return—his return to earth.

In the same way, Christ's return does not mean that he literally comes back to this earth. Rather, it means that he takes Kingdom power toward this earth and turns his attention to it. He does not need to leave his heavenly throne and actually come down to earth to do this.[20]

We have summarized the major teachings of the Watchtower Society concerning Jesus Christ. How do these teachings compare with the convictions of the early church fathers?

THE FATHERS AND THE DEITY OF CHRIST

Are the Witnesses correct in their doctrine of the nature of Christ? They are certainly not alone in denying his deity. Many world religions and men of great intellect have argued over the centuries that Jesus was merely human. Sometimes they have used the Scriptures themselves to substantiate their arguments. Is the belief held by the Christian church for nearly two thousand years, that Jesus is not only man but also God, a corruption brought about by the influx of paganism into Christianity during the first three centuries of its history, as the Watchtower Society has repeatedly and forcefully argued over its hundred-year history?

If the gospel were corrupted during the early centuries of the church, that should be readily discernible in the writings of those who were teachers and leaders at the time. But if not, then their writings should present abundant evidence of their belief in the deity of Christ. Documentation of this belief would certainly be most critical in the interval between the death of the apostles and the Council of Nicaea in 325, when the full, coequal deity of the Son with the Father was pronounced to be an unequivocal tenet of orthodox Christian faith.

Jehovah's Witnesses maintain that a great apostasy took place rapidly in the period immediately after the death of the apostles, leaving nothing but a paganized leadership throughout the nominal Christian church. Hence, they say, little evidence of the true faith remains in the writings of the early church fathers. They base this belief on the existence of doctrinal error and Gnostic influence in the churches addressed by the apostolic epistles, such as Paul's letter to the Colossians. This shows, they say, that apostasy began very early in church history.

Such a notion becomes untenable, however, when scrutinized at any length. It requires that nowhere in the evangelized world of the first and second centuries, from Egypt to Spain and beyond, in the churches established by the apostles and in the leadership appointed personally by them, was the true faith transmitted faithfully. This theory requires an extraordinary event: the simultaneous loss of faith by an entire generation of Christians throughout the civilized world. Included in this apostasy would be those thousands of martyrs who refused to deny Christ and worship pagan gods.

A great apostasy, had it occurred, would have begun in areas where pagan influence was greatest, where the church was accepting a large number of pagan converts. We should see the earliest corruption of doctrine in places such as Alexandria, where Greek philosophy was influential. The prominent Western churches established by the apostles, such as those in Rome and Antioch, would have fallen into heresy much more slowly. If a great apostasy had begun right after the apostles died, a mixture of true Christianity and pagan heresy should be observable in the writings of the early church.

Another possibility, of course, is that all the writings of the followers of the "true faith" were destroyed by the paganized church at a later date. But that is highly implausible, since texts have survived from the earliest and

31

most vigorously refuted heresy, Gnosticism. Many Gnostic writings, including a number of Gnostic gospels, have survived to the present day despite several centuries of concerted attack and condemnation by the church. The survival of not a single document supporting the Watchtower gospel therefore serves as an ample refutation of it. Keep in mind that the Watchtower organization's purpose in Jehovah's plan is to provide "meat in due season," that is, literature that explains the divine plan not otherwise discernible in the Bible. Where is the Watchtower literature of the first and second centuries? Surely the authentic church leaders wrote prolifically to provide the faithful with an understanding of the Scriptures, for the Witnesses maintain that the Scriptures themselves without such aids cannot be comprehended.[21]

The last and most compelling argument against the occurrence of a universal early apostasy is provided by the commissioning and empowering of the apostles themselves. If an abrupt postapostolic apostasy did occur, the apostles must have been incompetent evangelists, who utterly failed to accomplish Jesus' commission to make disciples of all men. Such an apostasy would speak poorly of Jehovah God as well, whose "holy spirit" was unable to preserve the purity and truth of his church for even a single generation after the apostles.

Tertullian, the great lawyer and apologist of the Western church at the end of the second century, succinctly argued against those who taught that the whole church had drifted into false doctrine.

> Grant, then, [if some have taught error] that all have erred; that the Apostle was mistaken in bearing witness; that the Holy Spirit had no such con-

sideration for any one Church as to lead it into truth, although He was sent for that purpose by Christ, who had asked the Father to make Him the Teacher of truth; that the Steward of God and Vicar of Christ neglected His office, and permitted the Churches for a time to understand otherwise and to believe otherwise than [Christ] Himself had preached through the Apostles: now, is it likely that so many and such great Churches should have gone astray into a unity of faith?[22]

With these things in mind, a careful examination of the writings of the early church is in order. An in-depth study of the entire body of early Christian literature is beyond the scope of a work such as this, and therefore quotations have been kept brief. Every effort has been made to insure that no quotation has been taken out of context; where necessary, the surrounding context has been provided. The reader is encouraged to study the original works themselves wherever possible. A substantial number of good modern translations are available, and they are listed in the bibliography.

CLEMENT OF ROME

Clement was a disciple of Paul and Peter, and may have been the person mentioned by Paul as a faithful fellow worker in Philippi (Phil. 4:3). He served as the bishop of the church at Rome, third in succession after the apostle Peter.[23] He was described by Irenaeus as a man strong in the tradition and teaching of the apostles.

He had seen the apostles and associated with them, and still had their preaching sounding in his ears

33

and their tradition before their eyes—and not he alone, for there were many still left in his time who had been taught by the apostles.[24]

Clement is best known for his epistle to the church at Corinth, which was written, as were Paul's letters to this church, in response to bitter divisions among its members. It was written at the close of Diocletian's persecution, about 95. Since Peter and Paul were martyred about 65, Clement's epistle was written about thirty years after their death. It was distributed and read throughout the church, and it was often read along with the Scriptures at the Eucharistic meal.[25] Some manuscripts from the Eastern church even include the letter along with the Scriptures. Clement wrote:

> The scepter of God's majesty, the Lord Jesus Christ, did not come with the pomp of pride or arrogance, though he could have done so. But he came in humility, just as the Holy Spirit said of Him.[26]

Clement describes Christ as the scepter of God's majesty, alluding to his power, authority, and sovereignty. He declares that Jesus, though possessing the majesty of God, did not come as one who was proud and arrogant, as he might rightfully have come, but rather as one who was humble. While this is not a direct statement of Christ's deity, in the context of his writing it strongly implies equivalence. This is reflected in another statement by Clement.

> For this is how Christ addresses us through his Holy Spirit: "Come, my children, listen to Me, I will teach you the fear of the Lord."[27]

Here Clement is introducing a series of Scripture quotations encouraging believers to abandon evil and pursue good. He identifies Christ as the speaker of the words of Scripture, through the Holy Spirit. This is a clear declaration of Christ's deity, for Jewish theology and apostolic teaching always maintained that God Himself was the author of Scripture (2 Tim. 3:16). Hence, Clement's epistle supports traditional Christian teaching about Christ, although it does not directly address the issue.

SECOND CLEMENT

A second epistle has also been attributed to Clement, although contemporary scholars regard it as the work of someone else. The so-called *Second Letter to the Corinthians* is an ancient homily by an unknown author, and it has been reliably dated between 120 and 140.[28] The author opens with this exhortation,

> Brothers, we ought to think of Jesus Christ as we do of God—as the "Judge of the living and the dead."[29]

Later in the homily, while speaking of the importance of obedience to Christ, the author says:

> But how do we acknowledge Him? . . . [B]y honoring Him [Christ] not only with our lips, but with all our mind and our heart. And He says in Isaiah as well, "This people honors me with their lips, but their heart is far from me."[30]

35

Here the author exhorts his listeners to honor Christ by worshiping him with their whole heart and their whole mind—as Jesus himself (quoting Deut. 6:5) commanded men to worship God (Matt. 22:37). He then attributes the words of Isaiah 29:13 to Jesus. This is yet another testimony that the early church believed Christ to be the author of the Scriptures and therefore equal with the Lord God.

THE SEVEN EPISTLES OF IGNATIUS

Ignatius served as head of the church at Antioch, a congregation that was second only to Rome in prominence. He lived at the close of the first century and in the early years of the second, and he was therefore a contemporary of Clement of Rome. According to tradition, he was a disciple of Peter, Paul, and John, and was established by them as bishop of Antioch.

Ignatius stands out in the early church as one of its most prominent and zealous martyrs. After being tried before a Roman governor in Antioch in 108 and condemned to be thrown to the wild beasts at Rome, he was transported through Asia Minor in chains as an object lesson to the Christian communities there, accompanied by a Roman guard. While en route, he wrote a series of seven letters, mostly to churches along the way, but also to the Roman church and to Polycarp, bishop of Smyrna.[31]

Ignatius is the most outspoken of the early Christian fathers in declaring the deity of Christ. Writing to the church at Ephesus, he begins,

> The source of your unity and election is genuine suffering which you undergo by the will of the Father and of Jesus Christ our God.[32]

36

Bold declarations that Jesus is God sound repeatedly through this beautiful epistle. The believers in Ephesus are encouraged to live a life in keeping with their high calling, "being imitators of God, and having your hearts kindled in the blood of God."[33] The "blood of God" can only refer, of course, to that of Jesus. Many other such statements are evident:

> There is one only physician—of flesh yet spiritual, born yet unbegotten, God incarnate, genuine life in the midst of death, sprung from Mary as well as God . . . Jesus Christ our Lord.[34]

> Let us therefore do all things as knowing that He dwelleth in us, to the end that we may be His temples and He Himself may be in us as our God.[35]

> For our God, Jesus the Christ, was conceived in the womb by Mary . . . of the Holy Ghost.[36]

> From that time forward every sorcery and every spell was dissolved . . . when God appeared in the likeness of man unto newness of everlasting life.[37]

The other epistles of Ignatius are no less resolute in their declaration of the nature of the Lord for whom he was in chains, and for whom he so eagerly sought martyrdom. In addressing the church established by Peter and Paul at Rome, he writes:

> Ignatius . . . to the church that is beloved and enlightened through the will of Him who willed all things that exist, by faith and love towards Jesus Christ our God . . . [38]

For our God Jesus Christ, being in the Father, is the more plainly visible.[39]

Permit me to be an imitator of the passion of my God.[40]

Similarly, in his letter to the Christians at Smyrna, he says:

I give glory to Jesus Christ the God who bestowed such wisdom upon you.[41]

Let no man be deceived. Even the heavenly beings and the glory of the angels and the rulers visible and invisible, if they believe not in the blood of Christ [who is God], judgment awaiteth them also.[42]

Ignatius also wrote to Polycarp, the bishop of Smyrna, who had been a disciple of the apostle John. In closing, Ignatius said, "I bid you farewell as always in our God, Jesus Christ."[43] Both Ignatius and Polycarp shared a faith acquired directly from the apostles. This is indeed a powerful testimony to apostolic teaching on the nature of Jesus Christ.

POLYCARP

Polycarp's understanding of Christ can also be discerned from two other documents. He, like Ignatius, suffered a martyr's death, which is detailed in a remarkable and touching letter written to the church at Smyrna shortly after his death in 155. Polycarp also wrote an epistle to the church at Philippi, in response to a request by them for copies of any letters of Ignatius that he might have in his possession. Taking this opportunity to encourage them to forgive one another, Polycarp writes:

> If, then, we pray the Lord to forgive us, we our-selves ought also to forgive; for we are before the eyes of the Lord and God, and we must all stand at the judgment seat of Christ. . . . So then, let us "serve Him with fear and all reverence," as He him-self has commanded, and also the apostles who preached the gospel to us and the prophets who foretold the coming of the Lord.[44]

The reference to "the Lord" can only be to Christ, as there is mention of his commands to the apostles and his coming judgment of men. Polycarp concludes his epistle with the following prayer, further confirming his belief in the deity of Christ.

> Now may the God and Father of our Lord Jesus Christ, and the eternal High Priest Himself, the [Son of] God Jesus Christ, build you up in faith and truth . . . and may He grant unto you a lot and a portion among His saints . . . who shall believe in our Lord and God Jesus Christ and in His Father that raised Him from the dead.[45]

The detailed and deeply moving account of Poly-carp's martyrdom lends further credence to his belief in the deity of the Son of God. After being arrested during a persecution of Christians at Smyrna, Polycarp stood before the magistrate, threatened with death by fire. He refused to reject the Lord whom he had served all his life.

> But when the magistrate pressed him hard and said, "Swear the oath, and I will release thee; revile the Christ," Polycarp said, "Fourscore and six years I have been His servant, and He hath done me no wrong. How then can I blaspheme my King who saved me?"[46]

Blasphemy can refer only to irreverence toward God himself, for the Christian holds no other gods or beings in the same light.

Following the dramatic description of Polycarp's death by fire, the author alludes to the reverence with which the remains of the martyrs were held. But he is careful to distinguish between the respect that the early church had for its martyrs and the adoration that is due to God alone:

> So he put forward Nicetes, the father of Herod and brother of Alce, to plead with the magistrate not to give up his body, "lest," so it was said, "they should abandon the crucified one and begin to worship this man." . . . They did not know that it will be impossible for us either to forsake at any time the Christ who suffered for the salvation of the whole world . . . or to worship any other but Him. For Him, being the Son of God, we adore, but the martyrs as disciples and imitators of the Lord we cherish, for they are worthy of this for their unequaled love for their King and Teacher.[47]

Hence it is clear, from both his own writing and the depiction of his heroic death, that Polycarp viewed Christ as fully God in the flesh. And those who wrote of his martyrdom to the churches of the second century shared his belief.

THE EPISTLE OF BARNABAS

This epistle was first cited by Clement of Alexandria, who understood the composition to be the work of Barnabas, the companion of the apostle Paul. The letter was held in high esteem by many of the early church fathers, and its authorship is ascribed to the apostolic Barnabas by later writers such as Origen, Eusebius, and Jerome. It was widely read and respected in the churches, along with other postapostolic writings, and it was considered by some in the early church to be part of the inspired Scriptures. While modern literary criticism has undermined the contention that Paul's companion Barnabas was its author, the epistle nevertheless stands as a work of considerable historical, doctrinal, and apologetic value.

The letter likely originated in Alexandria, a key center of Christianity in the East. While it is quite antagonistic to legalistic Judaism, it holds the Scriptures of the Old Testament in the highest esteem. Authorities date the letter as early as shortly after the fall of Jerusalem in A.D. 70.

Barnabas makes no unequivocal statements of Christ's deity, although this is strongly implied throughout. He does, however, testify to the nature of his resurrection. In this he concurs with all the patristic writers, that Jesus was raised bodily from the dead.

41

> Set your hope on Him who is about to be mani-
> fested to you in the flesh, even Jesus. . . . For they
> shall see Him in that day wearing the long scarlet
> robe about His flesh, and shall say, "Is this not He,
> Whom we once crucified and regarded as nothing
> and spat upon; verily this was He."[48]

Barnabas therefore offers no support for the notion
that Jesus was raised a spirit creature, without his human
flesh.

THE EPISTLE TO DIOGNETUS

The work known as the *Epistle to Diognetus* is an early
Christian apology, a defense of Christianity. When the
manuscript was discovered, it was initially believed to be
a later work by Justin Martyr. It is now attributed to an
unknown author, and dates from about 150. The work is
elegant and beautifully written. It is addressed to a certain
Diognetus, who was a philosopher and may have been the
tutor of the Emperor Marcus Aurelius in his youth. It was
apparently written in response to an inquiry from Diognetus about the Christian faith.

As he explains the basis of Christianity to this pagan
philosopher, a man well versed in Greek religious speculation, the writer takes great pains to explain how Christianity is different:

> On the contrary, it was really the Ruler of all, the
> Creator of all, the invisible God himself, who from
> heaven established the truth, and the holy, incom-
> prehensible word among men, and fixed it firmly

in their hearts. Nor, as one might suppose, did he do this by sending to men some subordinate—an angel, or principality, or one of those who administer earthly affairs, or perhaps one of those to whom the government of heaven has been entrusted. Rather he sent the Designer and Maker of the universe Himself. . . . God sent him to men.[49]

The author is alluding to the Gnostic view of the spiritual world and its interaction with the physical. The Gnostics believed the spiritual world to be good and the physical world to be evil, the two being separated by an insurmountable gulf. God dealt with the physical world through a series of angelic intermediaries who were given areas of responsibility over the various heavenly and earthly realms. Gnostic theology held that one of these angelic intermediaries, the Logos, came to earth as the Savior to set men free by revealing a higher knowledge (*gnosis* in Greek) to the enlightened. The apologist declares that Christianity does not believe the Logos to be an inferior angelic being, but rather One who was equal to the inapproachable God himself. He emphasizes this by calling both the Father and Christ the Creator of the universe, for the Greeks believed God alone to be the Creator.

Speaking of man's lack of knowledge about God prior to the coming of Christ, he says:

He [the Father] sent him [Christ] as God; He sent him as man to men. . . . [B]efore he came, what man had any knowledge of God at all? . . . And yet if any of these lines of argument [about God being equated with created elements] is acceptable, then each and every one of the other creatures could in

43

the same way shown to be God. . . . No man has ever seen God or made him known, but he has manifested himself.[50]

The apologist sees Jesus as the very manifestation of the invisible God, revealing him to men as no mere man or created thing could do. Furthermore, he draws a sharp distinction between the foolish speculation of the pagans, who equated God with the elements (such as fire), and he who revealed himself in his Son—the uncreated God himself.

The heart of the gospel, the message of a salvation offered freely to man by faith rather than by works, through the substitutionary death of Christ for our sins, rings out clearly from the pages of this epistle,

Then, when we had shown ourselves incapable of entering the kingdom of God by our own efforts, we might be made capable of so doing by the power of God. . . . God did not hate us, or drive us away, or bear us ill will. Rather, he was longsuffering and forbearing. In his mercy he took up the burden of our sins. He Himself gave up His own Son as a ransom for us—the holy for the unjust, the innocent for the guilty, the righteous one for the unrighteous, the incorruptible for the corruptible, the immortal for the mortal.[51]

How different this gospel is from that of the Watchtower Society, which proclaims a gospel of salvation through works and unswerving subservience to a human organization! The Society's "gospel" is absent from this epistle, as it is from all other writings of the early church.

It is nowhere to be found. The true gospel is heard repeatedly, however—that God "took upon Himself our sins, . . . the immortal for the mortal," as this epistle so eloquently states.

> I am not speaking of things that are strange to me, nor is my undertaking unreasonable, for I have been a disciple of apostles, and now I am becoming a teacher of the Gentiles. . . . This is he who was from the beginning, who appeared new and yet was found to be old, and is ever born young in the hearts of the saints. This is the eternal one, who today is accounted a Son.[52]

Thus ends the epistle, basing its teachings (as do all the patristic writings) on the authority of apostolic teaching, with the clear and unequivocal declaration of the eternal Logos, who is without beginning or end. The Jesus of the Watchtower Society, a created angel inferior to the Father, would surely have been strange and heretical to this disciple of the apostles and defender of the faith.

Justin Martyr and the Apologists

As Christianity won converts among the well-educated Greeks, there arose a series of Christian authors who turned their rhetorical skills to the defense of their new faith. From the character of their writings they are known as the apologists. They flourished during the reigns of the Roman emperors Hadrian, Antoninus Pius, and Marcus Aurelius, when Christianity was exposed to persecution and ridicule by the pagan world. The apologists refuted the charges and slanders of both Jews and Gentiles, vindicated the truths of the gospel, and attacked the errors and vices of idolatry. They were men of more learning and culture than the earlier apostolic fathers, as they were often philosophers and rhetoricians who had embraced Christianity at a mature age after earnest investigation. Their writings breathe the same heroism and enthusiasm for the faith that motivated the martyrs in their sufferings and death.

The most important and well known of the apologists was Justin Martyr. He was born into paganism at Flavia Neapolis in Palestine around 110, the son of gentile citizens of a Roman colony in Samaria. As a young man he attached himself successively to the various philosophical schools, including Stoicism and Platonism, and finally came to know Christianity. He eventually arrived in Rome, where he founded a school that produced many gifted apologists. He was beheaded, along with six companions, in 165. Justin was a prolific writer, but only two or three of his works (his two Apologies, which may have been one work, and his *Dialogue with Trypho the Jew*) have survived, along with a few fragments of his other writings.

Certain cautions are needed when using Justin's writings (or any of the apologists' works) to evaluate the beliefs and doctrines of the early church. Numerous authors over the years (including Jehovah's Witnesses) have quoted from the apologists and other church fathers in an attempt to show that Christians blended pagan philosophical concepts with early apostolic teachings to derive what became such orthodox Christian doctrines as the deity of Christ and the Trinity. These doctrines, it is claimed, were never taught, implicitly or explicitly, by Jesus or the apostles.

To respond to such arguments, some perspective on the apologists and their environment is needed. The apologists—and this is particularly true of Justin—were generally men who had come to the Christian faith after extensive exposure to Greek philosophy. They had discovered both intellectual and spiritual truth in the apostolic teachings of the Christian church, in sharp contrast to the empty pagan philosophies of their time. Having found the true philosophy and faith in Christianity, the apologists undertook to defend that faith to those with pagan beliefs. Hence, their arguments are often couched in terms and concepts that would be comfortable and readily understandable to the philosophically minded pagans whom they addressed, but which can be easily misconstrued by modern-day readers. This is especially true when passages are lifted out of their context, as is invariably done by the Witnesses and other contemporary assailants of Christianity.

When interpreting the apologists, and indeed all the patristic writers, it is important to recognize that their understanding of some doctrines of the Christian faith was incomplete, at least to a degree. Many difficult and complex issues, such as the relationship of the human and the divine in Christ and the relationship of the Son to the Father, were simply not the subject of a great deal of literary attention in Christianity's early years. It was not until alternative theologies emerged, challenging what the church intrinsically knew to be true, that men began to delve more deeply into such issues. For any one individual, such an investigation could and indeed did produce some variance from what the church ultimately accepted as orthodox belief. This tendency was most pronounced in those who were experienced in the philosophical speculation so prevalent at that time. The most notable (and some would say notorious) example of this was Origen, whose theological speculations where of such a magnitude that the Roman church declared him a heretic many years after his death. The church in time corrected those beliefs of *individuals* which varied from what *the body as a whole* agreed upon as the truth. Nevertheless, it is evident from a balanced reading of their works that the basic tenets of the Christian faith, which have been taught from the apostles to the present day, are repeated consistently, despite the occasional lapses that do arise.

At times, for example, the apologists and the Alexandrian fathers seem to imply a definite subordination of Christ or the Spirit, making them inferior to the Father. But when such statements are examined in the context of the entire work in which they appear, along with the author's other writings, they invariably are seen to portray the Son and the Spirit in a sense in which it is impossible to distinguish their characteristics from those of the Father himself. What is certain in every instance is that none of the apologists ever held an Arian or Russellite view of the Son. They would have regarded any doctrine portraying Christ as a created angel as a heresy worthy of the most vigorous rebuttal.

The largest and most important surviving work of Justin Martyr is his *First Apology*. Justin addressed this defense of the Christian faith to the Roman emperor and prominent philosophers of his day. Christians then were often accused of "atheism," for they refused to worship the emperor or Roman gods. Justin refutes this charge with a statement of the Christian faith in God.

> So we are called atheists. Well, we do indeed proclaim ourselves atheists in respect to those whom

you call gods, but not in regard to the Most True
God. . . . On the contrary, we reverence and worship Him and the Son who came from Him and
taught us these things, and the army of the other
good angels who follow him and are made like
him. The prophetic Spirit we also worship and
adore.[53]

Justin's statement is one that can easily be taken out
of context and interpreted to say that Jesus was created
like the angels who follow him "and are made like him."
The context demands just the opposite, however. Justin, in
response to the accusation of atheism, is asserting that
Christians worship the Father, and the Son who came from
him, and the prophetic Spirit. Certainly Justin is not pro-
moting polytheism, since he often speaks elsewhere of the
existence of but one God. Justin speaks of God as "the True
God"[54] and "the good and unbegotten God,"[55] and he con-
tinually refers to God in the singular. He also refutes the
notion that lesser angelic creatures, such as demons,
should be referred to as gods, saying that "the demons
who do such things are not only not rightly called gods,
but are in fact evil and unholy demons."[56]

Justin's portrayal of the Christian worship of God,
which includes worship of the Father, Son, and prophetic
Spirit, cannot then be construed as a reverence for lesser
"angelic" gods. Such worship would be entirely out of
keeping with the tone and thrust of his work, which
ridicules polytheistic pagan beliefs. The mention of the
holy angels in the midst of the delineation of the God
whom Christians worship is admittedly surprising. In the
context of the passage, it is most likely meant as a paren-
thetical contrast to the demons, who deserve no reverence

and cannot rightfully claim to be "gods" because of their moral wickedness. The angels, by contrast, are worthy of the reverence of man.

Having clarified what the Christian faith alone acknowledges as divine—the Godhead of Father, Son, and Spirit—Justin repeatedly emphasizes the divine nature of Christ throughout his *First Apology:*

> For what human laws could not do, that the Word, being divine, would have brought about, if the evil demons had not scattered abroad many false and godless accusations.[57]

> Although the Jews were always of the opinion that it was the Father of all who had spoken to Moses, it was in fact the Son of God, who is called both Angel and Apostle, who spoke to him. . . . They who assert that the Son is the Father are proved to know neither the Father, nor that the Father of all has a Son, who is both the first-born Word of God and is God.[58]

The last quotation is another passage that might be interpreted to mean that Jesus was no more than an angel—until it is examined fairly and in context. As we scrutinize Justin's argument, we see that he is identifying Christ as the Angel of the Lord who spoke from the flaming bush (Ex. 3:2)—and hence as the Lord himself (vv. 4, 6):

> What was said out of the bush to Moses, "I am He who is, the God of Abraham and the God of Isaac and the God of Jacob and the God of your fathers," was an indication that they though dead still ex-

50

isted and were Christ's own men. For they were the first of all men to devote themselves to seeking after God.[59]

In his *Dialogue with Trypho the Jew,* Justin clearly states what he believes about Christ's nature. Explaining to Trypho the limitations of logical arguments in communicating spiritual truth, Justin says,

Now certainly, Trypho . . . it is inescapable that this is the Christ of God, even if I am unable to prove to you that He preexisted as the Son of the Creator of things, being God, and that He was born a man by the Virgin.[60]

There can be no question, then, that Justin believed that Jesus was God in the flesh. Nor was he alone in this conviction among the defenders of Christianity.

ATHENAGORAS

All that is known about Athenagoras is that he was a Christian philosopher in Athens during the reign of Marcus Aurelius (161–80). He was a contemporary of Justin and Tatian the Syrian. In rhetorical ability he far exceeded Justin, writing in a very attractive Greek style. And whereas Tatian was given to a rather pugnacious contentiousness, Athenagoras showed great respect for those whom he hoped to influence.

Athenagoras addressed an apology, the *Intercession on Behalf of the Christians,* to the emperors Marcus Aurelius and Commodus. The *Intercession* is a defense against the capricious judgments to which Christians were subjected on account of their name alone, and particularly against the false accusations of atheism, cannibalism, and incest. He refutes these charges calmly, clearly, eloquently, and conclusively. Historians without exception have held him in high esteem as the most eloquent of the apologists. He declares:

> I have sufficiently demonstrated that we are not atheists, since we acknowledge one God. . . . We recognize also the Son of God. Let no one think it laughable that God should have a Son. For we do not conceive of either God the Father or the Son as do the poets, who, in their myth-making, represent the gods as no better than men. The Son of God is the Word of the Father . . . the Father and the Son being one. . . . [T]he Son . . . is the First-begotten of the Father, not as having been produced—for from the beginning God had the Word in Himself, God being eternal mind and eternally rational.[61]

With this eloquent and succinct statement, Athenagoras lays out the basis for the Christian faith in God, and the nature of that God, to the pagan emperors. Christians believe in one God, he argues, and hence are not atheists. Yet in the same breath he proclaims the sonship of the Word and his unity and eternal coexistence with the Father, and soundly refutes any notion that Christians believe the Only Begotten to be a creature, with a beginning in time. Does Athenagoras believe, then, that God is some sort of plurality of gods, thereby blending pagan polytheism with Christianity? Not at all, for he says:

If, moreover, it is claimed that, just as hand, eye, and foot are constituent parts of a single body, so God's unity is made up from two or more gods, this is equally false. . . . But God is uncreated, impassible, and indivisible. He does not, therefore, consist of parts.[62]

Athenagoras comes as close as anyone in the first three centuries to expressing the nature of the Godhead in terms that we are familiar with today. After emphasizing the unity and indivisibility of God, he proceeds to explain the nature of the Godhead:

The Son of God is his Word in idea and actuality; for by him and through him all things were made, the Father and the Son being one. And since the Son is in the Father and Father in the Son by the unity and power of the Spirit, the Son of God is the mind and Word of the Father. . . . [T]he Son . . . is the first offspring of the Father. I do not mean that he was created, for since God is eternal mind, he had his Word within himself from the beginning, being eternally wise. . . . Who, then, would not be astonished to hear those called atheists who admit God the Father, God the Son, and the Holy Spirit, and who teach their unity in power and their distinction in rank?[63]

Clearly, what Athenagoras believed about the nature of God and Christ differs in no material way from the doctrine of orthodox Christianity throughout the centuries.

IRENAEUS

While the apologists were confronting the external threat of the pagan government and its religious system, church leaders began writing polemical literature against heresies and various forms of pseudo-Christianity, especially Gnosticism. It was these works perhaps more than any other that initiated the development of dogmatic theology in the church. The earliest and most prominent figures in this group were Irenaeus and Hippolytus, both of whom received a Greek education but labored in the Western church.

Irenaeus was the last and most prominent of a series of gifted teachers and confessors from Asia Minor, the region where the apostle John last labored. These men, who included Polycarp of Smyrna, Papias of Hierapolis, and Melito of Sardis, formed a direct link to the apostle John, having studied under John himself or one of his disciples.

Irenaeus was born about 120 in Asia Minor and spent his youth in Smyrna. He was a disciple of Polycarp, the pupil of John, and he studied under other "elders," who were either immediate or second-generation disciples of the apostles. Irenaeus inherited the spirit of his preceptor. "What I heard from him," he says, referring to Polycarp, "I did not write on paper, but in my heart, and by the grace of God I constantly bring it afresh to mind."[64] After serving as a missionary to Gaul during a fierce persecution in 177, he was appointed bishop of Lyons in 178. His zeal as a writer and missionary was such that he is said to have converted nearly the entire city of Lyons, and he was instrumental in spreading Christianity throughout Gaul.

His most noted composition is the *Detection and Over-*

throw of the Gnosis Falsely So Called, usually called *Against Heresies*, a five-volume work composed between 177 and 190. Irenaeus is generally regarded as the most important theologian of this period, and his writings shed considerable light on both the faith of the church and the substance of Gnostic speculation during the latter part of the second century.

The first book of *Against Heresies* lays the groundwork for a rebuttal of Gnosticism by reiterating the faith passed down to the church from the apostles.

> Now the Church, although scattered over the whole civilized world to the end of the earth, received from the apostles and their disciples its faith in one God, the Father Almighty . . . and in one Christ Jesus, the Son of God, who was made flesh for our salvation, and in the Holy Spirit . . . in order that to Jesus Christ our Lord and God and Savior and King, in accord with the approval of the invisible Father, every knee shall bend of those in heaven and on earth and under the earth, and that every tongue shall confess Him.[65]

All of the church fathers judged teaching to be true and trustworthy if it originated in apostolic teaching, and Irenaeus was no exception. For him, Jesus was "our Lord and God," to whom every knee would ultimately bow. He believed, and declared as apostolic teaching, that Jesus was raised bodily and was received in the flesh into the heavenly glory of his Father. He did not understand the Word to be a product of the Father's creation; rather, he clearly set forth the creative power of the Word, who is himself uncreated.

> There is one almighty God, who formed all things
> through His Word, and fashioned and made all
> things which exist out of that which did not exist.
> About these things the Scripture says, "For by the
> Word of the Lord were the heavens established, and
> all their strength by the Spirit of His mouth." And
> again, "All things were made through Him, and
> without Him was made nothing." From all, how-
> ever, there is no exception; and the Father made all
> things through Him.[66]

Irenaeus here quotes Psalm 33:6, which testifies to the
creative acts of the Lord, and John 1:3, which speaks of the
creative acts of the Word (the Logos), and he applies both
passages to Christ. Furthermore, he emphasizes the exclu-
sivity of John 1:3—without exception, nothing has been
created except that which the Word himself created. Hence,
the Word himself cannot have been created.

This treatise focuses on the speculative fantasy of
Gnosticism. Gnostic sects often ascribed to the Logos a beginning, likening him, as the Word, to human speech,
which has a beginning when first spoken. Irenaeus would
have none of this, for it contradicted the teaching of the
apostles.

> [The Gnostics] transfer the generation of the ut-
> tered word of men to the eternal Word of God, at-
> tributing to Him a beginning of utterance and a
> coming into being in a manner like to that of their
> own word. In what manner, then, would the Word
> of God—indeed, the great God Himself, since He
> is the Word—differ from the word of man, were He
> to have the same order and process of generation?[67]

Irenaeus attributed the perfect words of Scripture, written by God himself, to the Word of God, Jesus Christ: "The Scriptures are certainly perfect, since they were spoken by the Word of God and by His Spirit."[68]

According to the Watchtower Society, Irenaeus believed that the prehuman Jesus was inferior to the Father. The booklet *Should You Believe in the Trinity?* represents Irenaeus as believing that Jesus was "not equal to the 'One true and only God.'"[69] The citation used to substantiate this was not taken from the works of Irenaeus, however. It was taken instead virtually word for word from a secondary source, in a paragraph that represents the summary and opinion of the author of that work.[70]

Even the most cursory reading of Irenaeus, however, refutes the Society's representation of his position. Consider these statements, just two of his many testimonies to the deity and coequality of the Son with the Father:

> What cannot be said of anyone else who ever lived, that He is Himself in His own right God and Lord and Eternal King and Only begotten and Incarnate Word, proclaimed as such by all the Prophets and by the Apostles and by the Spirit Himself, may be seen by all who have attained to even a small portion of the truth. The Scriptures would not have borne witness to these things concerning Him, if, like everyone else, He were mere man.[71]

> The Virgin Mary . . . being obedient to His word, received from an angel the glad tidings that she would bear God.[72]

This ancient saint provides the very words to refute those who would attempt to twist his teaching to their own ends, denying his Savior. He speaks their condemnation: "But not knowing Him . . . they are deprived of His gift, which is life eternal."[73] By proclaiming another Jesus, the Witnesses have failed to understand what "may be seen by all who have attained to even a small portion of the truth."

THEOPHILUS

Theophilus of Antioch was converted from heathenism by the study of the Scriptures. He occupied the episcopal see at Antioch, being the sixth in line from the apostles, during the latter part of the reign of Marcus Aurelius. He died about 181. Theophilus was the first of the fathers to use the term *triad* in reference to the Godhead. His principal work is a three-volume apology, *To Autolycus*, addressed to an educated heathen friend. His principal object is to convey to his friend the falsehood of idolatry and convince him of the truth of Christianity. Speaking of the nature of the Logos, he says:

> The divine Scripture itself teaches us that Adam said he had heard the voice. And what else is this voice, but the Word of God, which also is His Son,—not as poets and writers of myths tell of the sons of gods begotten of intercourse, but. . . . This is what the Holy Scriptures teach us, as do all the inspired men, one of whom, John, says, "In the beginning was the Word, and the Word was with God," showing that at first God was alone, and the Word was in Him. Then he says, "And the Word

was God; all things were made through Him, and without Him was made nothing." The Word, then, being God and being generated from God, is sent to any place at the will of the Father.[74]

This passage provides particularly compelling grounds for rejecting the notion that Watchtower Christology represents the belief of the early church. Not only is the voice in the Garden, the voice of God, clearly identified as that of the Word, but the unequivocal denial of any origin for the Logos is plainly stated. The context of this passage makes it apparent, without ambiguity, that Theophilus understood the Logos to be God, not some angelic pseudodeity. Like all the early Christian writers, Theophilus refers to the teachings of the apostles as the standard that validates his beliefs and the criterion against which they are to be measured.

MELITO OF SARDIS

Very little is known of Melito, the bishop of Sardis in Lydia, who died around 190. Although he was a prolific writer, only a few fragments of his works survive. One such fragment, from a work called *Guide*, gives us a glimpse of his understanding of Christ.

> The activities of Christ after His Baptism, and especially His miracles, gave indication and assurance to the world of the Deity hidden in His flesh. Being God and likewise perfect man, He gave positive indications of His two natures: of His Deity, by the miracles during the three years following af-

ter His Baptism; of His humanity, in the thirty years which came before His Baptism, during which, by reason of His condition according to the flesh, He concealed the signs of His Deity, although He was the true God existing before the ages.[75]

HIPPOLYTUS

Hippolytus was one of the most learned and eminent scholars and theologians of his time. He received an excellent Greek education and heard the discourses of Irenaeus, probably in Lyons or Rome. His public life fell at the end of the second century and the first three decades of the third (about 198 to 236). He belonged to the Western church, although he may have been of Greek extraction, like Irenaeus.

Hippolytus was a prominent presbyter in Rome and led a schismatic movement centered on doctrinal and disciplinary differences with the bishop of Rome. He died a martyr in the mines of Sardinia in 236. He was a voluminous writer, but unfortunately few of his writings have survived. His principal surviving work is a multivolume treatise called *Refutation of All Heresies*.

Hippolytus portrayed Christ in a clear and orthodox manner. There is no evidence that he believed him to be a created being. For Hippolytus, Jesus was God in the flesh. Despite attempts by the Witnesses in their recent literature to appropriate his teachings, the words of Hippolytus emphatically and unequivocally refute the Watchtower theology.

Only His Word is from Himself, and is therefore also God, becoming the substance of God.[76]

For Christ is the God over all, who has arranged to wash away sin from mankind, rendering the old man new.[77]

Let us believe . . . according to the tradition of the Apostles, that God the Word came down from heaven into the holy Virgin Mary. . . . He came forth into the world and, in the body, showed Himself to be God, although it was as perfect man that He came forth.[78]

The writings of Hippolytus do not support a theology that denies the deity of Jesus Christ. Assertions to the contrary betray either poor scholarship or dishonesty.

TERTULLIAN

Tertullian was born in Carthage of pagan parents between the years 155 and 160. He became a lawyer of considerable prestige, and after his conversion, around 193, his expert knowledge in the field of law was turned to the defense of Christianity. His writings were widely read throughout the church, due in no small part to his use of Latin (he was the first of the Fathers to write in this language). His style—vigorous, entertaining, and not infrequently acerbic—further contributed to his reputation and appeal.

Tertullian was solidly orthodox throughout most of his life, although in his later years he drifted into Montanism, a very ascetic sect with a strong emphasis on prophetic revelation. Tertullian's understanding of Christ is self-explanatory:

We hold that this which was uttered by God, and which was begotten in that utterance, because of the unity of substance is called God and Son of God; for God too is Spirit. . . . [Christ] was born God and man combined.[79]

God alone is without sin. The only man without sin is Christ; for Christ is also God.[80]

We do indeed believe that there is only one God. . . . He was sent by the Father into a Virgin and was born of her, God and man, Son of Man and Son of God, and was called by the name Jesus Christ.[81]

There is no evidence that Tertullian believed the Son to be an angel. Instead, he emphasizes his deity as a necessary prerequisite to man's salvation.

"But Christ," they say, "also bore the nature of an angel." For what reason? And why did He take human nature? . . . Christ bore human nature in order to be man's salvation. . . . [T]here was no such reason why Christ would take upon Himself angelic nature.[82]

Tertullian's brilliantly crafted prose and acerbic wit would have been directed in full measure against anyone who claimed that Jesus was merely a man, transformed at His birth from a created angelic being.

ORIGEN

Unequaled in intellectual brilliance and controversial as few others after his death, Origen stands out as a giant of the Eastern church during the first half of the third century. There are more biographical details available about him than about any of the earlier theologians, mostly because the sixth book of Eusebius's *Ecclesiastical History* is devoted almost entirely to him. He was born in 185 at Alexandria, a child of Christian parents. When his father, Leonidas, was martyred during the persecution of Septimius Severus, in the year 202, Origen's mother prevented her zealous son from accompanying him to martyrdom by the simple expedient of hiding his clothes. Under his direction—as a layman—the prestigious theological school of Alexandria reached its greatest prominence. During the Decian persecution he was tortured and imprisoned, and as a result of his sufferings he died at Tyre at the age of sixty-nine, in 253 or 254.

Disputes regarding the orthodoxy of Origen's doctrine never arose during his lifetime, but they did three times during the following three centuries. He was a great scholar and theologian, and he always strove to be orthodox in his faith. Yet, he finally came to be regarded as a heretic, which resulted in the destruction of the vast majority of his many writings and the corruption of much of what remained. Those areas of theological speculation considered most errant, however, dealt not with fundamental Christian doctrine, but rather with the preexistence of the soul. On core doctrine Origen never strayed from orthodoxy, nor was he ever accused of having done so.

Origen's essential beliefs about Christ are best seen in his treatise *Fundamental Doctrines*.

> The holy Apostles, in preaching the faith of Christ, treated with the utmost clarity of certain matters which they believed to be of absolute necessity to

all believers. . . . The specific points which are clearly handed down through the apostolic preaching [are] these: First, that there is one God who created and arranged all things. . . . Secondly, that Jesus Christ Himself, who came, was born of the Father before all creatures. . . . Although He was God, He took flesh; and having been made man, He remained what He was, God. . . . For we do not hold that which the heretics imagine: that some part of the substance of God was converted into the Son, or that the Son was procreated by the Father from non-existent substances, that is, from a substance outside Himself, so that there were a time when He did not exist.[83]

Certain of Origen's writings were later understood to imply the subordination, and therefore the inferiority, of the Son. It is clear from this passage, however, that Origen believed the Son to be fully God, equal with the eternal Father.

JESUS-CREATED ANGEL OR GOD BECOME MAN?

The quotations presented in this chapter are an extensive, but not exhaustive, sampling of the beliefs of the early church leaders and teachers. They span the era from the apostles to that generation which, at the Council of Nicaea, confirmed the coessential deity of the Father and the Son. Any impartial reading of the early church fathers will confirm the representative nature of these quotations. The reader is encouraged to validate their context and accuracy by investigating any of the numerous translations now available. There can be no doubt that the church consistently and unfailingly taught that Jesus Christ was God in human flesh; that he was not a created angel, but had eternally coexisted with the Father; that his resurrection was indeed a bodily one; and that he would likewise return in the flesh as God and man.

Perhaps even more striking than the testimonies of these early Christian scholars, martyrs, and pastors, is the absence of anything even faintly resembling the doctrines propounded by the Watchtower Society. This is equally true, incidentally, of the apocryphal and Gnostic literature of this period. The Watchtower gospel of Jehovah's kingdom, with Jesus/Michael as its angelic head, was not the dominant, or even a deviant, theology at any point in the postapostolic period. It is only with the rise of Arianism in the first part of the fourth century that anything remotely resembling Russellism can be discerned. This provides compelling evidence that Charles Russell's teachings and his organizational legacy are not those of the apostles or of those who preserved the Christian faith after them.

NOTES

1. *You Can Live Forever in Paradise on Earth* (Brooklyn: Watchtower Bible and Tract Society of New York, Inc., 1982), 39–40.
2. Walter R. Martin and Norman H. Klann, *Jehovah of the Watchtower* (Minneapolis: Bethany, 1974), 46.
3. Arius (ca. 250–336) taught that Jesus was a created being, inferior by nature to the Father. This belief was condemned as heresy by the Council of Nicaea in 325. Arianism and its relation to the teachings of the Witnesses are discussed in the next chapter.

4. Charles T. Russell, *Studies in the Scriptures*, vol. 5: *The At-One-Ment Between God and Man* (Brooklyn: International Bible Students Association, 1891), 84.
5. Ibid., 86, 88.
6. *You Can Live Forever*, 57–58.
7. *What Has Religion Done for Mankind?* (Brooklyn: Watchtower Bible and Tract Society of Pennsylvania, 1951), 231.
8. *You Can Live Forever*, 62.
9. Ibid., 63.
10. A class of "anointed" men known as "the 144,000" will receive spirit bodies and live in heaven, according to Watchtower theology.
11. Charles T. Russell, *Studies in the Scriptures*, vol. 1: *TheDivine Plan of the Ages* (Brooklyn: International Bible Students Association, 1886), 152.
12. *You Can Live Forever*, 52.
13. Harold O. Brown, *Heresies* (Grand Rapids: Baker, 1984), 51–53.
14. Kurt Rudolph, *Gnosis,* translation edited by R. McLachlan Wilson (San Francisco: Harper & Row, 1983), 160.
15. According to the doctrine of soul death no immaterial part of man (i.e., his soul or spirit) survives the terminal event; a person ceases to exist at the moment of death. A "resurrection" is thus the re-creation of the body. This doctrine will be explored in depth in chapter 5.
16. *Awake,* July 22, 1979, 27.
17. *You Can Live Forever*, 67.
18. Ibid., 144.
19. Ibid., 145–46.
20. Ibid., 147.
21. The Watchtower Society, while claiming to use the Bible alone, actually teaches that the Bible cannot be understood without the aid of the "meat in due season," i.e., the literature provided by the Society—its interpretation of the Scriptures being the only valid one. See *Watchtower,* Sept. 15, 1910, 298; ibid., Aug. 15, 1981, 28.

22. Tertullian, *The Demurrer Against the Heretics*, 28.1. William A. Jurgens, *The Faith of the Early Fathers*, vol. 1 (Collegeville, Minn.: Liturgical Press, 1979).

23. Philip Schaff, *History of the Christian Church*, vol. 2 (1910; reprint, Grand Rapids: Eerdmans, 1987): 637–38.

24. Irenaeus, *Against Heresies*, 3.3.3. Cyril C. Richardson, *Early Christian Fathers* (New York: Macmillan, 1970).

25. Eusebius Pamphilus, *Ecclesiastical History*, trans. Christian Frederick Cruse (1850; reprint, Grand Rapids: Baker, 1987), 4.23.11.

26. *1 Clement*, 16. Richardson, *Early Christian Fathers*.

27. Ibid., 22.

28. Schaff, *History of the Christian Church*, 2:648–49.

29. *2 Clement*, 1. Richardson, *Early Christian Fathers*.

30. Ibid., 3.

31. Schaff, *History of the Christian Church*, 2:653–55.

32. Ignatius, *Ephesians*, 1. Richardson, *Early Christian Fathers*.

33. Ibid.

34. Ibid., 7.

35. Ibid., 15. J. B. Lightfoot, *The Apostolic Fathers* (1891; reprint, Grand Rapids: Baker, 1956).

36. Ibid., 18.

37. Ibid., 19.

38. Ignatius, *Romans*, 1. Lightfoot, *The Apostolic Fathers*.

39. Ibid., 3.

40. Ibid., 6.

41. Ignatius, *Smyrnaeans*, 1. Lightfoot, *The Apostolic Fathers*.

42. Ibid., 6.

43. Ignatius, *Polycarp*, 8. Richardson, *Early Christian Fathers*.

44. Polycarp, *Philippians*, 6. Richardson, *Early Christian Fathers*.

45. Ibid., 12. Lightfoot, *The Apostolic Fathers*.

46. *Martyrdom of Polycarp*, 9. Lightfoot, *The Apostolic Fathers*.

47. Ibid., 17.

48. Epistle of Barnabas 6, 7. Lightfoot, *The Apostolic Fathers*.

49. *Epistle to Diognetus*, 7. Richardson, *Early Christian Fathers*.

50. Ibid., 7, 8.
51. Ibid., 9.
52. Ibid., 11.
53. Justin Martyr, *First Apology*, 5. Jurgens, *The Faith of the Early Fathers*, vol. 1.
54. Ibid., 13.
55. Ibid., 14. Richardson, *Early Christian Fathers*.
56. Ibid., 5.
57. Ibid., 10.
58. Ibid., 63. Jurgens, *The Faith of the Early Fathers*, vol. 1.
59. Ibid.
60. Justin Martyr, *Dialogue with Trypho the Jew*, 48. Jurgens, *The Faith of the Early Fathers*, vol. 1.
61. Athenagoras, *Intercession on Behalf of the Christians*, 10. Jurgens, *The Faith of the Early Fathers*, vol. 1.
62. Ibid., 8. Richardson, *Early Christian Fathers*.
63. Ibid., 10.
64. Irenaeus, *Epistle to Florinus*, quoted in Eusebius Pamphilus, *Ecclesiastical History*, 5.20.
65. Irenaeus, *Against Heresies*, 1.10.1. Richardson, *Early Christian Fathers*.
66. Ibid., 1.22.1. Jurgens, *The Faith of the Early Fathers*, vol. 1.
67. Ibid., 2.13.8.
68. Ibid., 2.28.2.
69. See Appendix 1.
70. See Appendix 2.
71. Irenaeus, *Against Heresies*, 3.19.1–2. Jurgens, *The Faith of the Early Fathers*, vol. 1.
72. Ibid., 5.19.1.
73. Ibid.
74. Theophilus, *To Autolycus*, 2.22. Jurgens, *The Faith of the Early Fathers*, vol. 1.
75. Melito, *Guide*, 13. Jurgens, *The Faith of the Early Fathers*, vol. 1.
76. Hippolytus, *Refutation of All Heresies*, 10.33. Jurgens, *The Faith of the Early Fathers*, vol. 1.

77. Ibid., 10.34.
78. Hyppolytus, *Against the Heresy of a Certain Noetus*, 17. Jurgens, *The Faith of the Early Fathers*, vol. 1.
79. Tertullian, *Apology*, 21.13. Jurgens, *The Faith of the Early Fathers*, vol. 1.
80. Tertullian, *The Soul*, 41.3. Jurgens, *The Faith of the Early Fathers*, vol. 1.
81. Tertullian, *Against Praxeas*, 2.1. Jurgens, *The Faith of the Early Fathers*, vol. 1.
82. Ibid., 14.1.
83. Origen, *Fundamental Doctrines*, 1. pref. 2–4; 1.2.1; 4.4.1. Jurgens, *The Faith of the Early Fathers*, vol. 1.

4

The Holy Spirit and the Trinity

Charles Russell, writing in 1911 with the conviction that "the subject of the holy Spirit . . . has been grievously misunderstood by many of the Lord's people for centuries," sought to set the record straight, for "in the light of the *parousia* [the invisible presence of the Lord] . . . this subject is becoming more clear and reasonable, as it evidently was to the early Church."[1] Russell taught:

> Equally consistent is the Scripture teaching respecting the holy Spirit—that it is not another God, but the spirit, influence, or power exercised by the one God, our Father and by his Only Begotten Son.

[T]here is absolutely no ground whatever for thinking of or speaking of the holy Spirit as another God,
distinct in personality from the Father and the Son.
. . . From the foregoing we perceive that a broad
definition of the words "Spirit of God" or "holy
Spirit," would be—the divine will, influence, or
power.[2]

Thus was launched the Watchtower doctrine of the
"holy spirit," which the Society continues to disseminate
in its literature today. Armed with the certainty that the
doctrine of the Trinity is pagan in origin, having been introduced into the church in the second century as a result
of the "great apostasy," the Jehovah's Witnesses continue
to maintain that the orthodox Christian understanding of
the Spirit is incorrect and "against reason."

The current doctrine of the Holy Spirit put forth by
the Watchtower Society differs in no material respect from
that of Charles Russell.

The Bible's use of "holy spirit" indicates that it is
a controlled force that Jehovah God uses to accomplish a variety of his purposes. . . . No, the holy
spirit is not a person and it is not part of a Trinity.
The holy spirit is God's active force that he uses to
accomplish his will. It is not equal to God but is always at his disposition and subordinate to him.[3]

The Bible says: "They all became filled with holy
spirit." Were they "filled" with a person? No, but
they were filled with God's active force. . . . How
could the holy spirit be a person, when it filled
about 120 disciples at the same time?[4]

The personal descriptions that the Scriptures give to the Holy Spirit, such as "Comforter" and "Helper," are dismissed by the Society. As the reference work *Insight on the Scriptures* explains:

> Personification Does Not Prove Personality—It is true that Jesus spoke of the holy spirit as a "helper" and spoke of such helper as "teaching", "bearing witness", "giving evidence", "guiding." . . . [I]t is not unusual in the Scriptures for something that is not actually a person to be personalized or personified. Wisdom is personified in the book of Proverbs.[5]

Similarly, the Society understands the use of masculine pronouns with reference to the Spirit, a feature especially prominent in John's gospel, to be merely an appropriate use of grammar, not evidence of personality.

> Hence we have in John's use of the masculine personal pronoun in association with *pa-ra'kle-tos* an example of conformity to grammatical rules, not an expression of doctrine.[6]

Does this teaching about the Holy Spirit correspond to that of the apostolic and postapostolic church? Did the "clear and reasonable" understanding of the Spirit by the early church really parallel the postulates of Russell and the Society that he founded? The Society believes so, for it declares:

> Not until the fourth century C.E. did the teaching that the holy spirit was a person and part of the "Godhead" become official church dogma. Early

church "fathers" did not so teach; Justin Martyr of the second century C.E. taught that the holy spirit was an "influence or mode of operation of the Deity"; Hippolytus likewise ascribed no personality to the holy spirit.[7]

What did the early church fathers actually say about the Holy Spirit? Did they consider the Spirit to be personal or impersonal? Did those writing in the shadow of the apostles ever consider the Holy Spirit to be the equal of God himself?

An examination of writings of the early church fathers reveals that scant literary attention was paid to the Holy Spirit, and even less was paid to the Spirit's nature and personality. Most allusions to the Spirit in the early church writings are peripheral and tangential; there is no early author who devotes any significant attention to the issues of the Spirit's nature, personality, or deity. The paucity of material on the Spirit raises questions of its own. Was teaching about the Holy Spirit considered important in the Christian church? Was the subject of the Spirit relatively minor, or was it rather an integral and indispensable part of the apostolic faith? Since so little was written about the Spirit, can it even be determined with certainty whether the Spirit was considered to be personal or impersonal? Only by examining the postapostolic writings themselves can we begin to gain sufficient insight to answer these questions.

THE HOLY SPIRIT IN THE WRITINGS OF THE EARLY CHURCH

Most references to the Spirit in early Christian literature follow the pattern of the baptismal formula of

Matthew 28:19, where the Father, the Son, and the Holy Spirit are mentioned together without any elaboration. This formula appears frequently, sometimes in baptismal instruction manuals, at other times in declarations of faith or allusions to Scripture.

> Pour water on the head thrice in the name of the Father and of the Son and of the Holy Spirit.[8]

> For as God lives, and as the Lord Jesus Christ lives and the Holy Spirit (on whom the elect believe and hope). . . . [9]

> "Do you believe in God, the Father Almighty? . . . Do you believe in Christ Jesus, the Son of God, who was born of the Holy Spirit? . . . Do you believe in the Holy Spirit and the holy church and the resurrection of the flesh?" . . . Then, pouring the consecrated oil into his hand and imposing it on the head of the baptized, he shall say: "I anoint you with holy oil in the Lord, the Father Almighty and Christ Jesus and the Holy Spirit."[10]

Such references contribute little to our understanding of how these writers perceived the nature of the Spirit. At best they suggest that the Holy Spirit was held in equal esteem with the Father and the Son, an implication quite significant in light of the convictions of the Fathers about the deity of Jesus. However, little certainty can be attached to an inference based on such citations alone.

The Spirit is commonly mentioned in early Christian literature in passages that are rich in imagery and allegory. One theme frequently presented in this manner in the New

Testament and the postapostolic literature is the indwelling of God within the regenerate heart. This profound truth is dimly glimpsed in the types and symbolism of the tabernacle in the Old Testament, but it echoes repeatedly and clearly throughout the New Testament. The Old Testament picture of the tabernacle, and later the temple, where God dwelt among men, is carried forward in the New Testament in numerous references to the indwelling of God, the Lord Jesus, and the Spirit within the bodily temple of the believer.[11] The authors of the earliest church letters and apologies expressed the joyful conviction that God dwelt within their hearts and those of their listeners, and they used this fact repeatedly to exhort their flocks to live lives consistent with this marvelous gift.

The so-called Epistle of Barnabas (written by an unknown author) uses this imagery extensively. Written shortly after the fall of Jerusalem in A.D. 70, this epistle was prominent among the early church writings, discussing the relationship of the Old Testament to the Christian faith. While the unbelieving Jews are treated harshly in this epistle, it deals lovingly and carefully with the Old Testament itself, seeing everywhere in it types and prophecies of the New Covenant in Christ. The author's frequent use of the Jewish temple as a type is indeed revealing.

> Behold then we have been created anew, as He said again in another prophet, "Behold, says the Lord, I will remove from them," that is to say, from those whom the Spirit of the Lord foresaw, "their stony hearts and will put into them hearts of flesh." For He Himself was to be manifested in the flesh and to dwell in us. For the abode of our heart, my brothers, is a holy temple to the Lord.[12]

Before we believed on God, the abode of our heart was corrupt and weak, a temple truly built by hands. . . . By receiving the remission of our sins and hoping on the Name we became new, created afresh from the beginning. Therefore God dwells truly in our dwelling within us. . . . He Himself [is] dwelling in us. . . . For he that desires to be saved looks not to man, but to Him that dwells and speaks in him. . . . This is the spiritual temple built up to the Lord.[13]

Barnabas develops the Old Testament concept of the temple, applying it to the new life of the believer in Christ. The image of the temple at Jerusalem was vivid in the mind of the author, for it had been destroyed by the Romans only a short time before he wrote his epistle. For the Jews, the temple was the very dwelling place of God among men. Here God was approached: the Shekinah (the glory of the Lord) was present within. Here, in the most sacred Holy of Holies, the high priest annually presented the propitiatory sacrifice for the sins of the people. God himself resided here in his magnificence and holiness.

Barnabas expands on the New Testament concept of the Christian as the temple of God. He exhorts his listeners to perfect God's new temple, the heart of the believer, by aspiring to spiritual perfection through sanctification. Discussing the new creation in the first passage quoted above, Barnabas cites Ezekiel 11:19, which speaks of the new heart of flesh to be given by the Lord. Who then will "dwell in us," in this heart of flesh? "He Himself," the Lord God "manifested in the flesh"—that is, Jesus (a powerful testimony, by the way, to Barnabas's belief in the deity of

Jesus Christ). There is a sense in which the "Spirit of the Lord," the Lord God, and Jesus (the Lord "manifested in the flesh") are interchangeable in this passage. Furthermore, the action attributed to the Spirit implies personality. Could an impersonal power "like electricity" *foresee* those whose hearts would be transformed?

Barnabas is not alone in alluding to the indwelling of God within the human heart, nor in speaking of the heart of the believer as a temple, the dwelling place of God. The unknown author of *2 Clement* writes, in the early second century, "We ought therefore to guard the flesh as a temple of God."[14]

In a similar passage, the author of the *Epistle to Diognetus* speaks of the presence of the eternal Word within the hearts of the saints. He does not specify the Spirit directly, but he illustrates the interchangeability with which the early fathers spoke of the Father, the Spirit, and the Word dwelling within the heart of Jesus' followers.

> This Word, Who was from the beginning, Who appeared as new and yet was proved to be old, and is engendered always young in the hearts of saints, He, I say, Who is eternal, Who today was accounted a Son . . . [15]

Ignatius, one of the church's most revered martyrs, who so repeatedly and lucidly speaks of the deity of Christ, also testifies to the indwelling of God the Father and of Jesus Christ in the temple of the believer. While he does not mention the Spirit directly in such a context, his testimony bears witness to the fundamental conviction of the early church—that God was present in the heart newly created through faith.

I realize that you are not conceited; for you have
Jesus Christ in yourselves.[16]

Let us, then do everything as if He were dwelling
in us. Thus we shall be His temples, and He will
be within us as our God—as he actually is.[17]

One of the most widely read and esteemed writings
of the early postapostolic age was a lengthy work known
as the *Shepherd of Hermas*. Ancient tradition maintains that
the author was a friend of Paul—the Hermas to whom he
sends greetings in Romans 16:14. This tradition readily accounts for the high authority accorded to this work in the
early church. According to the book itself, it was written
late in the author's life, when he was a contemporary of
Clement, the presbyter-bishop of Rome at the close of the
first century.

The *Shepherd of Hermas* has a unique literary form
among the writings of the postapostolic fathers. It is an allegory, strongly emphasizing Christian morality and calling the church to renewed fervor in light of the approaching Day of Judgment. Because of Hermas's close relationship with Clement, the *Shepherd* is thought to reflect closely
the faith of the church at Rome at the end of the first century.

Hermas refers to the Spirit more frequently than any
other father, although, like theirs, his references tend to be
incidental. Certain passages do indicate his understanding
of the nature of the Spirit, however, and that gives us a
glimpse of the early church's understanding in this area.

Love truth, and let nothing but truth proceed out
of thy mouth, that the Spirit which God made to

79

dwell in this flesh, may be found true in the sight of all men; and so shall the Lord, Who dwelleth in thee, be glorified.[18]

For if thou art long-suffering, the Holy Spirit that abideth in thee shall be pure, not being darkened by another evil spirit, but dwelling in a large room shall rejoice and be glad within the vessel in which he dwelleth.[19]

Take heed therefore, ye that serve God and have Him in your heart: work the works of God being mindful of His commandments and of the promises which He made, and believe Him that He will perform them, if His commandments be kept.[20]

Hermas here talks of "the Spirit which God made to dwell in this flesh," and in a parallel manner he states that "the Lord" dwells within the Christians whom he is addressing, thereby equating the Spirit and the Lord. Since the Lord is personal, we may infer that Hermas understood the Spirit to be both personal and divine. The striking interchange of references to God, the Lord, and the Spirit as the One who dwells in the human heart gives powerful testimony to the coequality with which the triune personalities were understood by Hermas and the church at the end of the first century. So Hermas, the friend of Paul and the contemporary of Clement, shows no evidence of understanding the Spirit in any way akin to the teaching of the Watchtower Society.

The writers of Scripture attributed actions to the Holy Spirit that are normally associated with personality, and the early Christian writers continued this practice. In the patristic literature, the Spirit is often portrayed as speaking, especially through the medium of the Scriptures.

> He [the Lord] saith again in another prophet: "Behold, saith the Lord, I will take out from these," that is to say, from those whom the Spirit of the Lord foresaw, "their stony hearts and will put into them hearts of flesh," for He Himself was to be manifested in the flesh and to dwell in us.[21]

> The Spirit saith to the heart of Moses, that he should make a type of the cross and of Him who was to suffer, that unless they set their hope upon Him, war will be waged against them for ever.[22]

> Either they [the followers of the heretic Artemon] do not believe that the Sacred Scriptures were uttered by the Holy Spirit, and they are thus infidels, or, they deem themselves wiser than the Holy Spirit, and what alternative is there but to pronounce them demoniacs?[23]

The Holy Spirit is depicted as having a will and choice, as when he assigns the titles of the Son, in Justin Martyr's *Dialogue with Trypho the Jew.*

> "Friends," I said, "I will give you another testimony, from the Scriptures, that God begot before all creatures a Beginning, who was a certain Rational Power from Himself, and whom the Holy Spirit calls the Glory of the Lord, or sometimes the Son, sometimes Wisdom, sometimes an Angel, sometimes God, sometimes Lord and Word."[24]

81

The Spirit is depicted as a teacher and a preacher.

> But He in whom I am bound is my witness that I
> learned it not from flesh of man; it was the preach-
> ing of the Spirit who spoke on this wise.[25]

> The Holy Prophetic Spirit taught us this when He
> informed us through Moses that God spoke as fol-
> lows to the first created man: "Behold, before your
> face, the good and the evil. Choose the good."[26]

The *Shepherd of Hermas* uses an enlightening parallel,
which reveals the author's understanding of the nature of
the Spirit.

> He that has the [divine] Spirit, which is from above,
> is gentle and tranquil and humble-minded, and ab-
> staineth from all wickedness and vain desire of this
> present world, and holdeth himself inferior to all
> men, giveth no answer to any man when enquired
> of, nor speaketh in solitude (for neither doth the
> Holy Spirit speak when a man wisheth Him to
> speak); but the man speaketh then when God
> wisheth him to speak.[27]

At first this passage seems ambiguous about the nature of the Holy Spirit, for it describes the character of a
man who has received "the divine Spirit, *which* is from
above." This could certainly refer to the impersonal power
of God. However, the passage goes on to remove any such
possibility, saying that the Spirit does not speak at man's
insistence, but rather that man speaks at God's command.
This implies that the Spirit has an independent will and

an ability to speak, both of which are personal character-istics. Furthermore, both the Spirit and God are said to be behind the man's speech, which makes the Spirit and God equivalent.

Virtually all of the attributes that we associate with a personal being are attributed to the Spirit by the early fa-thers. Note in the following passages how the Spirit man-ifests emotion; how he functions as an intermediary be-tween two personal beings, God and man, by intercession; how he exercises endurance and accuses sinners; how he proclaims the truth of God without deception. It is surely stretching the limits of plausibility to maintain that this is simply the literary personification of an impersonal power or force. To see such consistent personification would be particularly unlikely across the wide spectrum of literary styles and forms seen in the writings of the fathers.

> The doubtful mind saddens the Spirit, because it succeeded not in its business, and the angry temper again, because it did what was evil. Thus both are saddening to the Holy Spirit. . . . Put away there-fore from thyself sadness, and afflict not the Holy Spirit that dwelleth in thee, lest haply He intercede with God [against thee], and depart from thee.[28]

> The Jews . . . were rightly censured both by the Prophetic Spirit and by Christ himself, since they knew neither the Father nor the Son.[29]

> Neither does Scripture falsify anything, nor does the Holy Spirit deceive His servants, the prophets, through whom He is pleased to announce to men the will of God.[30]

83

The Watchtower Society maintains that the early fathers understood the Spirit to be an impersonal power emanating from God. They quote Justin Martyr as teaching that the Holy Spirit "was an 'influence or mode of operation of the Deity.'" And they maintain that "Hippolytus likewise ascribed no personality to the holy spirit."[31]

The origin of the Society's quote from Justin Martyr is unclear, since it is not footnoted, and nothing similar to this statement appears in the limited manuscripts of Justin's work available to us. In his *First Apology*, the largest of his works, Justin uses the term "prophetic Spirit" twenty-four times and refers to the "Divine Spirit" twice. The remainder of the references to the Spirit are quotes from Scripture or references to the baptismal formula of Matthew 28:19. In none of these instances does he speak of the Spirit as an "influence or mode of operation," nor does this phrase appear in his *Second Apology*, the *Dialogue with Trypho the Jew*, *The Resurrection*, or *Exhortation to the Greeks*. In fact, the opposite impression is gained by reviewing Justin's depiction of the Spirit in these works. The prophetic Spirit is worshiped;[32] he announces;[33] he predicts;[34] he speaks through the prophets;[35] he speaks through Christ;[36] he exhorts;[37] he teaches;[38] he foretells;[39] he testifies;[40] he censures the unbelieving Jews, along with Christ.[41] Perhaps the statement most similar to the Watchtower quote is found in the *First Apology*, and it completely contradicts the Watchtower assertion. Justin, speaking of the miraculous conception of Jesus, says:

> The Spirit and the Power from God cannot rightly be thought of as anything else than the Lord, who is also the First-born of God, as Moses the above-mentioned prophet testified. So this Spirit, coming

upon the Virgin and overshadowing her, made her pregnant—not by intercourse, but by divine power.[42]

Another possible source for this quote is the *Dialogue with Trypho the Jew*, where Justin says,

I will give you another testimony, from the Scriptures, that God begot before all creatures a Beginning, who was a certain Rational Power from Himself, and whom the Holy Spirit calls the Glory of the Lord, or sometimes the Son, sometimes Wisdom, sometimes an Angel, sometimes God, sometimes Lord and Word.[43]

Here the reference is obviously to Christ as the Logos, not to the Spirit, and it bears powerful testimony to Justin's belief in the deity of Christ.

Did Hippolytus, as claimed by the Society, deny the personal nature of the Spirit? The vast majority of references to the Spirit in the writings of Hippolytus are indeterminate on this subject. Most of his references to the Spirit are found in his *Apostolic Tradition*, which was written about 215. This work provides a considerable body of information on the liturgy and organization of the early church. Numerous references to the Spirit are present in it, but these lie within the framework of the liturgical orders and the baptismal formula, and they provide no clue to the early church's belief regarding the personality of the Spirit. What few clues we do have from Hippolytus on this subject suggest that he, and the church of his time, understood the Spirit as a personal being, not an impersonal power or force.

Neither does Scripture falsify anything, nor does the Holy Spirit deceive His servants, the prophets, through whom He is pleased to announce to men the will of God.[44]

For either they do not believe that the Sacred Scriptures were spoken by the Holy Spirit, in which case they are unbelievers, or, if they regard themselves as being wiser than the Holy Spirit, what else are they but demoniacs?[45]

There is insufficient evidence in the writings of Hippolytus to make dogmatic statements about his view regarding the Spirit's personality. What little evidence we do have, however, does not support the Watchtower Society's conclusions.

Summarizing the doctrine of the Holy Spirit in early Christian writings, several conclusions may safely be reached. First, it is apparent that no highly developed theology of the Holy Spirit was in place in the first several centuries of church history. New believers were baptized into the faith by declaring their belief in the Father, the Son, and the Holy Spirit, yet no formal exposition of the nature and deity of the Spirit is seen in the early patristic writings. The Holy Spirit is frequently mentioned in these works, as either the voice of the Scriptures, or the guidance behind the Old Testament prophets, but his precise relationship to the Son and the Father is not delineated. We simply do not know the exact understanding of the ante-Nicene fathers on this subject.

But throughout these writings there runs a strong undercurrent depicting the Spirit in a manner far different from the Society's portrayal. References to the Spirit as an impersonal force or energy of God are virtually unseen. With the exception of a few questionable statements by Origen and Clement of Alexandria, who were prone to speculative philosophical theology (and even they acknowledge the Spirit's deity and personality), all of the ante-Nicene fathers spoke of the Spirit in personal terms, as having emotions, will, speech, and character. The ease with which they could speak interchangeably of God, the Son, and the Spirit as the inhabitant of the human heart strongly indicates that they hold to the orthodox belief in the deity of the Spirit. It is certainly not overstepping reasonable bounds to conclude that the early Christian writings depict the Holy Spirit in a fashion far more in harmony with present orthodox teaching than with the theology of Charles Russell and his followers.

THE WITNESSES AND THE TRINITY

Since the Jehovah's Witnesses deny the personality and deity of the Holy Spirit, along with the deity of Jesus, it comes as no surprise that they reject the orthodox Christian doctrine of the Trinity, as well. Indeed, they are especially vitriolic in their contempt for the Trinitarian Godhead, and have been since the time of Charles Russell.

> The general thought of Christendom is greatly perplexed by what is known as "The doctrine of the Trinity," a doctrine which its most pronounced advocates admit they do not understand and cannot comprehend or explain. . . . They declare in one breath that there is only one God . . . yet in the same breath they declare that there are three Gods (be-

cause to this theory they are committed by "the traditions of the fathers" handed down from the earliest Papacy).[46]

The Trinity is considered to be "one God in three Persons." Each is said to be without beginning, having existed for eternity. Each is said to be almighty, with each neither greater nor lesser than the others. Is such reasoning hard to follow? Many sincere believers have found it to be confusing, contrary to normal reason, unlike anything in their experience. How, they ask, could the Father be God, Jesus be God, and the holy spirit be God, yet there be not three Gods but only one God?[47]

Should Christians believe in the Trinity? Is the doctrine of the triune God, hated and demeaned by Russell and the Society he founded, a teaching unknown to the early church, brought into the faith by political intrigue and Constantine's pagan influence? How can contemporary Christians reconcile the lack of early trinitarian development, so exploited by the Witnesses, with their conviction that the Father, the Son, and the Spirit are coequal and coeternal members of the Godhead, and with their certainty that such a belief is scriptural and apostolic in origin?

Jehovah's Witnesses delight to argue the subject of the Trinity. They are quick to point out that the word *trinity* does not appear in the Bible, and they eagerly demonstrate that the doctrine in its present form was not formulated until the latter part of the fourth century—two assertions that are undeniably true. From this they conclude, marshaling numerous resources for verification, that the doctrine of the Trinity is of pagan origin, a God-dishonoring travesty that should be rejected by all who serve Jehovah in truth.

Christians are often ill at ease discussing and defending the doctrine of the Trinity, particularly in the face of such a well-organized attack. They instinctively and experientially know that Jesus is God and have confidence that the Spirit is personal and equal with the Father. Yet they are hard-pressed to respond to the formidable historical facts that seemingly conspire against them. If indeed history is a strong witness against the trinitarian formulation, and if the apostles and the early church had no such convictions, then modern orthodox Christianity is truly on shaky ground.

THE HISTORICAL DEVELOPMENT OF THE DOCTRINE OF THE TRINITY

The word *trinity* is indeed absent from the pages of Scripture, and it does not appear in the patristic literature until Tertullian uses it in about 200. The absence of this word from the Scriptures, however, should pose no difficulty for any Christian defending his faith, as the term is a purely functional one. The word *trinity* expresses the church's belief in the full, uncreated deity of God the Father, Jesus Christ, and the Spirit—coeternal, coequal, yet individually distinct. The Witnesses themselves use a number of such nonbiblical function words, such as *theocracy*, and thus they can hardly object to the fact that *trinity* is another such term.

The historical development of the trinitarian formulation is a considerably more complex matter. The church endeavored for some time to come to terms with the nature of the Godhead, particularly trying to reconcile the deity of Christ with Christianity's monotheistic Judaic roots. In a very real sense, the record of the church during its first three centuries is a chronicle of faith preceding knowledge, of a protracted grappling with the nature of God and the Savior. The struggle was propelled by heretical movements, which put forward alternative explanations of the nature of Christ, and, to a much lesser extent, of the Spirit. As such teachings were neutralized with apostolic doctrine tailored to the specific challenge, the church came to understand the triune God more fully. The doctrine of the trinity was not the result of pagan speculative thought; rather, it was the product of defending the apostolic faith against just such speculation. Early church history is the record of a growing understanding of God through the defense of his truth.

An examination of the history and writings of the early church reveals an extended period of controversy. Dissension was present virtually from the origin of the faith. The Jewish core of early Christianity taught that Jesus was the Messiah and that his death was the basis for the forgiveness of sins, but it provided few insights into the manner in which Jesus might be both man and divine Savior. Paul testifies frequently to the deity of Christ (see, for example, Rom. 10:9–13; Phil. 2:6; Titus 2:13); yet even at this formative point in the church's history, such an assertion faced opposition. At the heart of Paul's dispute with Jewish Christians about the law was the deity of Christ and the personhood of the Spirit. By proclaiming the teachings of Jesus and the testimony of the Spirit as the equivalent of the Old Testament law, the apostle was effectively claiming that the law uttered from Sinai by the

Lord himself was no longer the supreme and unique revelation of God. According to the apostles, a revelation of God himself, different in nature from his law, had taken place in the person of Jesus. The apostles further understood this revelation to be manifest in the church through the presence of the Holy Spirit (Acts 5:3, 4).

Controversy over this revelation of God did not cease with the passing of the apostles; rather, it escalated, centering on the relationship of the divine and the human in Christ. At one extreme were the Ebionites, a Jewish-Christian sect. Being committed to Old Testament monotheism, they denied both the divinity of Christ and his virgin birth. They considered Jesus to be the Messiah only by virtue of his strict observance of the law. Such legalism proved little different from Judaism itself, adding only a human Jesus as the Messiah.

Other factions tried to fit Jesus in with the religious syncretism prevalent among intellectual Hellenistic Jews of the late first century. One such group, the Elkesaites, represented a type of Jewish Christianity marked by theosophical speculations and strict asceticism. Rejecting the virgin birth of Christ, they nevertheless spoke of him as a higher spirit or angel. Jesus was regarded as an incarnation of the ideal Adam and was referred to as the highest archangel.

Opposition to apostolic teaching came also from another perspective: the denial, not of the deity of Jesus, but rather of his humanity. This denial characterized the widespread religious phenomenon known as Gnosticism. The dualistic worldview of Gnosticism condemned all material things as base and corrupt, and could not accept that a spiritual, divine being would have taken a human nature. Accordingly, Gnostic speculation formulated a Logos who, while divine by nature (actually, one of many gods), was human only in semblance or appearance. This approach satisfied the longing of the Greek mind for a fuller understanding of the mysteries of the Incarnation, and it had great appeal for the elite and the intellectual—those who found a Savior who was both human and divine unreasonable, and a gospel of the cross an insult to their wisdom.

The Gnostics presented a formidable challenge to orthodox Christianity in the early part of the second century. Gnosticism was not purely or even primarily a Christian heresy, but rather a religious and philosophical movement that combined elements of Eastern mysticism with Greek philosophical speculation. Yet there were elements of Gnostic thought that straddled Christian belief or borrowed from it in an attempt to define the nature of the Logos and the Sophia (Wisdom or Spirit) and their relationship to the unknowable Father. Such speculations were indeed far from the faith and understanding of the apostles. Gnosticism was nevertheless instrumental in initiating a process whose outcome clarified the nature of the triune God. The church, responding to the denial of Christ's deity by the Jew and the rejection of his humanity by the Gnostic, affirmed the full humanity and full deity of the Logos made flesh, thereby laying the foundation for the development of the doctrine of the Trinity.

The tension between the humanity and the deity of Christ continued in various forms for several centuries. The latter part of the second century brought Monarchianism, a movement arising out of the need to reconcile the divinity of Christ with the unity of God. The Monarchians believed that any distinction of persons in the Godhead necessitated some degree of subordination. Such subordination, they believed, was incompatible with the concept of one God.

Two main forms of Monarchianism developed, Adoptionism and Modalism. Adoptionism held that Jesus was a man who possessed impersonal power that issued from God, a power that came upon him at his baptism, when God adopted him as his Son. Modalism, on the other hand, maintained that the Father, Son, and Holy Spirit were three "modes" or manifestations of one God, rather than three distinct persons. Modalists believed that the Father was born as Jesus Christ, and that he died and raised himself from the dead. Neither of these formulations was satisfactory to the church. Adoptionism maintained the unity of the Godhead by sacrificing the deity of Christ; Modalism maintained it by sacrificing the separate personality of the Son and the Spirit. The church recognized these formulations to be heretical, and they were combated vigorously by Tertullian, Hippolytus, and Origen.

Theology in the third century was dominated by Origen, the Alexandrian whose deeply intellectual writings had no parallel in the early church. Origen's brilliance produced works of such depth and complexity that they inadvertently sowed seeds of further disputes over the nature of Christ. This confusion was fostered by scattered references that seemed to imply that the Son was subordinate in nature to the Father. The complexity of Origen's thought gave rise to controversies that culminated in the great Arian debate of the fourth century.

Arius, an Alexandrian presbyter, proposed in 318 that the Son was created. He maintained that if the Father had begotten the Son, then the Son must have had a beginning, and hence that there must have been a time when the Son did not exist. Arianism was a subtle heresy, which seem-

93

ingly had an answer for every difficult question concerning the nature of Christ. Gerald Bray, in his work *Creeds, Councils, and Christ,* says of Arius's teaching:

> Its spiritual power lay in the attractiveness of having a saviour who was like us (as a creature) yet more powerful (because he was a divine being). It avoided the crude adoptionism of Paul of Samosata, who had taught that Jesus was a mere man, without so far identifying Jesus with God as to make it impossible for him to experience human suffering and death.[48]

Arianism became popular for its simplistic appeal, and its adoption by a number of prominent political and religious figures gave rise to a bitter and divisive struggle in the church. The Council of Nicaea in 325, called by Emperor Constantine to resolve the dispute, decisively stated the orthodox position that Jesus was both fully divine and fully human, "true God from true God," "of one substance with the Father." Nevertheless Arianism thrived, especially in the Eastern church, for nearly fifty years after the council's proclamation.

Not unexpectedly, the Nicene declaration of the Son's full equality with the Father gave rise to a reevaluation of the nature and role of the Holy Spirit in the Godhead. The Spirit, having received virtually no theological attention prior to Nicaea, now became the focus of intense investigation and no little controversy. Arius had taught that the Holy Spirit was the first being created by the Son. In contrast, Athanasius, the great defender of the faith against the Arians, held the orthodox view that the Spirit was one in essence with the Father. Others, such as Macedonius, maintained that the Spirit was a creature subordinate to the Son. Ultimately, due in large part to the great scholars Basil of Caesarea, Gregory of Nyssa, and Gregory of Nazianzus, the full deity and coequality of the Spirit was formally recognized as orthodox Christian doctrine at the Council of Constantinople in 381.

THE WITNESSES AND NICAEA

Jehovah's Witnesses, along with many others who attack the doctrine of the Trinity, direct much of their onslaught against the creeds of Nicaea and Constantinople. The Watchtower booklet *Should You Believe in the Trinity?* is representative, giving this background on the Council of Nicaea:

> For many years there had been much opposition on Biblical grounds to the developing idea that Jesus was God. To try to solve the dispute, Roman emperor Constantine summoned all bishops to Nicea. About 300, a fraction of the total, actually attended. . . . Constantine himself presided, actively guiding the discussions, and personally proposed . . . the crucial formula expressing the relation of Christ to God in the creed issued by the Council, "of one substance with the Father." . . . Overawed by the emperor, the bishops, with two exceptions only, signed the creed, many of them much against their inclination. Hence, Constantine's role was crucial. . . . [T]his pagan politician intervened and decided in favor of those who said that Jesus was God.[49]

95

The accuracy of this portrayal demands verification, for if the doctrine of the coequal deity of Christ were politically imposed on the church by imperial coercion, this might indeed undermine its validity. Fortunately, a number of documents from eyewitnesses to the council have survived, against which this hypothesis can be tested. The most significant of these have been brought together in *A Historical View of the Council of Nice,* by Isaac Boyle.

According to such contemporaries as Eusebius, the bishop of Caesarea, who was actually a moderate at the council, the controversy over the teachings of Arius had become so heated and divisive that Constantine, in an effort to bring peace to the church, called a general council to resolve the matter. Some 320 bishops from all over the Christian world assembled in Nicaea, along with a great number of lesser church leaders. Boyle, quoting Eusebius and Theodoret, leaves no doubt that this was a significant portion of the church leadership from throughout the Christian world.

> The pastors of three churches founded by the apostles were present.... "The most distinguished ministers of God met together from every part of Europe, Asia, and Africa." ... Others were esteemed on account of their past sufferings in the cause of our holy religion, still bearing in their bodies ... "the marks of the Lord Jesus."[50]

Even though the majority of the bishops who attended the council were from the Eastern church, and therefore more likely to be favorably disposed to the Arian position, the Watchtower Society's contention that their acceptance of the coequal deity of Christ resulted from imperial intimidation is refuted by the eyewitness accounts.

Early in the council, the Arians introduced their own statement of faith, a straightforward document plainly denying the deity of Christ. Eusebius describes the reaction of those attending the assembly.

> The bishops, assembled as they were from so many different and widely separated countries, stopped their ears on hearing such language, and rejected this doctrine as remote and alien from that of the Church. . . . A letter of Eusebius of Nicomedia [a prominent bishop who espoused Arianism] was read to the council, which contained the heretical opinion [the Arian teachings]. . . . [I]t excited so much indignation that it was rent in pieces. . . . The Arians also presented to the council a confession of faith, which was torn on being read, and pronounced to be spurious and false. A great outcry was raised against them, and they were generally accused of having betrayed the truth.[51]

The Synodical Epistle, written at the conclusion of the council by the assembled bishops to the church of Alexandria, provides a similar account of the proceedings.

> The impiety and iniquity of Arius and his associates was inquired into. . . . It seemed good to all, that his ungodly opinion should be anathematized, and the blasphemous words and expressions which he made use of. . . . All this was condemned by the Holy Synod, who could not patiently listen to a

doctrine so impious or absurd, and to language so blasphemous.[52]

Jehovah's Witnesses vigorously attack the council's declaration that the Son is of one substance (*homoousios*) with the Father. They criticize the term as nonscriptural and dismiss it for originating with a pagan emperor. While it is true that Constantine—who had embraced Christianity thirteen years earlier (a fact confirmed by his letters to church leaders during the Arian controversy)—urged the council to use the term *homoousios* to describe the relationship of the Son to the Father, it is enlightening to examine the circumstances that resulted in its acceptance and use.

The bishops at Nicaea placed great emphasis on the use of scriptural terms to delineate the nature of Christ.

The council wishing to set aside the terms employed by the Arians, and to use words authorized by scripture, said that our Lord was by nature the only Son of God, the alone Word, power and wisdom of the Father, true God, according to St. John; the splendor of the glory, and the image of the substance of the Father, as St. Paul writes.[53]

The followers of Arius, seeking to avoid rejection by the council as heretics, initially considered accepting this wording. They hoped to be accepted as orthodox, without altering their theology, by accepting the council's scripturally based definition while reinterpreting the cited passages to conform with their views. The Arians, for example, initially acquiesced in the statement that the Son was "the image of the substance of the Father." Conspiring among themselves, they concluded that since man was also said to be made in the image of God, such a statement could be accepted while still denying the uncreated deity of Christ. But the bishops at the council, preempted the Arians' cunning maneuver by removing any ambiguity in their language.

> The bishops . . . explained . . . by saying that the Son was of the substance of God. It is true, they remarked, that creatures are said to be from God, because they exist not of themselves, . . . but the Son alone is properly of the substance of the Father.[54]

> By the expression "consubstantial with the Father" nothing else is intended, than that the Son of God has no similitude with created beings, but resembles in all things the Father only, by whom He was begotten, and that He is of no other substance or essence than that of the Father . . . since we knew that some of the most learned and distinguished of the ancient bishops and writers had made use of the term consubstantial [*homoousios*], in treating of the divinity of the Father and the Son.[55]

Hence, the use of the term "one substance" or "consubstantial," while recommended by Constantine, was accepted by the bishops as an orthodox term of long standing—in lieu of a directly scriptural description—only because of the sophistry of the Arians. The term was judged a necessity under these circumstances to clarify the teaching and understanding of the apostolic church in contrast to the teaching of the Arians, who had attempted to infuse scriptural terms with meanings foreign to the teachings of Christ and the apostles.

The outcome of the council testified to the widespread conviction that Christ was consubstantial with the Father. Ultimately, only two of the 320 voting members, both Arians, refused to accept the formulation declaring the full deity of the Son, which forms the basis of the doctrine of the Trinity. Boyle summarizes the impact of this decision.

> The remarkable unanimity of the synod on the subject of our Savior's true and proper divinity . . . may be considered a powerful confirmation of the truth of this important doctrine. Every part of the Christian world was virtually represented by men who, from their commanding station and favorable opportunities, must be supposed to have been well acquainted with . . . the doctrine of the apostles on this important article of our faith. Most of them . . . lived within two centuries of the death of St. John. Could the original doctrine have been lost in a period so comparatively short? Could it have been corrupted? Could it have been generally corrupted throughout the Church?[56]

Following the council, Arianism continued to thrive for a period of time, particularly in the Eastern church—indeed, for a period of time it became the dominant position. It was fostered by the political intrigue of various bishops and the occasional support of certain emperors. The movement became increasingly divided, however, and within 150 years of the Council of Nicaea it was essentially dead.

Arianism is of particular historical significance in any study of the Jehovah's Witnesses, for their Christologies are very similar. Arius believed that there was only one uncreated God. The Son (or Logos), he said, had a beginning, having been created by the Father, and hence was neither eternal nor of the divine essence. This first and greatest of all created beings was brought into being so that through him the world might be created. Jesus was chosen by God because of his obedience and was called the Son of God in view of his future glory. Arius believed that Jesus was capable of virtue or vice, but obediently chose virtue. Christ was rightly venerated by men, but only on account of his adoption as God's Son.

These views are virtually indistinguishable from those held by Charles Russell and the Society he founded. Arius sought scriptural support in those passages which seem to represent the Son as inferior to the Father, such as Proverbs 8:22, Matthew 28:18, Mark 13:32, Luke 18:19, John 5:19; 14:28, and 1 Corinthians 15:28—verses commonly used today by Jehovah's Witnesses to support the inferiority and creation of the Son. It comes as little surprise, then, that the Society holds such contempt for the Council of Nicaea, for the council condemned the very theology upon which the Watchtower Society rests.

WATCHTOWER SCHOLARSHIP ON THE DEVELOPMENT OF THE DOCTRINE OF THE TRINITY

The Watchtower Society's leadership encourages individual Witnesses to accept its teachings as "meat in due season" and to trust the scholarship of the anonymous authors of its literature. Individual study of the Bible or outside sources independent of the organization is discouraged.

We may think of study as hard work, as involving heavy research. But in Jehovah's organization it is not necessary to spend a lot of time and energy in research, for there are brothers in the organization who are assigned to do that very thing, to help you who do not have so much time for this, these preparing the good material in the *Watchtower* and other publications of the Society.[57]

The Watchtower booklet *Should You Believe in the Trinity?* traces the development of the doctrine of the Trinity. It quotes a number of the ante-Nicene fathers to support the contention that this doctrine was unknown to the early church. In order to give a fair review of the Society's position, I wrote to them, asking where these quotations came from, since the sources are not given in the booklet. In response, I received a letter from the Society, along with photocopies of selected pages from a book entitled *The Church in the First Three Centuries*, by Alvan Lamson, published in 1869.[58] The quotations from the ante-Nicene fathers in the booklet were taken directly from this book, and in several instances statements quoted as patristic are the editorial opinions of Lamson himself. It is apparent from his writing that he was a Unitarian, set on proving that the doctrine of the Trinity was Platonic in origin and late in development. Lamson often uses partial quotations taken out of context to "prove" his point.

While it is not surprising that the Society would use a source in harmony with its own beliefs, any conscientious Witness should be deeply disturbed by the shoddy scholarship involved. The *Trinity* booklet uses a single, highly biased, secondary source for its patristic testimony while trying to give the impression that primary sources have been carefully researched. Such dishonesty does not speak well for an organization claiming to be God's prophet on earth, and it should warn Jehovah's Witnesses not to blindly trust their leadership to do their research for them.

THE FATHERS AND THE DOCTRINE OF THE TRINITY

While it is accurate to say that the *formal* doctrine of the Trinity did not exist prior to the Council of Nicaea, it is clear from the patristic literature that the ideas brought together in that doctrine—the deity and distinct personality of the Father, the Son, and the Holy Spirit— were nearly universally accepted by church leaders during that period. Some individual authors did tend to subordinate the Son to the Father, but there is simply no conclusive evidence from the body of early Christian literature that the uncreated deity of Christ or the personality and deity of the Spirit were ever seriously questioned, much less denied. Converted philosophers such as Justin Martyr and Clement of Alexandria often tailored their theological arguments to suit their pagan audiences, which left some of their statements when taken out of context, open to misinterpretation. However, their work, when taken as a whole, is consistent with and supportive of the orthodox faith accepted by Christians today. By contrast, no author prior to Arius in the fourth century developed a theology of the Son and the Spirit even remotely similar to that of Charles Russell and the Watchtower Society.

NOTES

1. Charles T. Russell, *Studies in the Scriptures*, vol. 5: *At-One-Ment Between God and Man* (Brooklyn: International Bible Students Association, 1891), 165.
2. Ibid., 165, 169, 182.
3. *Should You Believe in the Trinity?* (Brooklyn: Watchtower Bible and Tract Society of Pennsylvania, 1989), 20, 23.
4. *You Can Live Forever in Paradise on Earth* (Brooklyn: Watchtower Bible and Tract Society of New York, 1982), 40, 41.
5. *Insight on the Scriptures* (Brooklyn: Watchtower Bible and Tract Society of New York, 1988), 2:1019.
6. Ibid.
7. Ibid.
8. *Didache*, 7. J. B. Lightfoot, *The Apostolic Fathers* (1891; reprint, Grand Rapids: Baker, 1956).
9. *1 Clement*, 58. Cyril C. Richardson, *Early Christian Fathers* (New York: Macmillan, 1970).
10. Hippolytus, *Apostolic Tradition*, 21, 22. William A. Jurgens, *The Faith of the Early Fathers*, vol. 1 (Collegeville, Minn.: Liturgical Press, 1979).
11. John 14:17; Rom. 8:9, 11; 1 Cor. 3:16, 17; 6:19; 2 Cor. 6:16; 13:5; Gal. 2:20; Col. 1:27; 2 Tim. 1:14; 1 John 4:4, 13, 15, 16.
12. *Barnabas*, 6. Lightfoot, *The Apostolic Fathers*.
13. Ibid., 16.
14. *2 Clement*, 9. Richardson, *Early Christian Fathers*.
15. *Epistle to Diognetes*, 11. Lightfoot, *The Apostolic Fathers*.
16. Ignatius, *Magnatians*, 12. Richardson, *Early Christian Fathers*.
17. Ignatius, *Ephesians*, 15. Richardson, *Early Christian Fathers*.
18. Hermas, *Mandates*, 3.1. Lightfoot, *The Apostolic Fathers*.
19. Ibid., 5.1.
20. Hermas *Similitudes*, 1. Lightfoot, *The Apostolic Fathers*.
21. *Barnabas*, 6. Lightfoot, *The Apostolic Fathers*.
22. Ibid., 12.
23. Hippolytus, *The Little Labyrinth*, quoted in Eusebius Pam-

philus, *Ecclesiastical History*, trans. Christian Frederick Cruse (1850; reprint, Grand Rapids: Baker, 1987), 5.28.15, 18. Jurgens, *The Faith of the Early Fathers*, vol. 1.

24. Justin Martyr, *Dialogue with Trypho the Jew*, 61. Jurgens, *The Faith of the Early Fathers*, vol. 1.
25. Ignatius, *Philippians*, 7. Lightfoot, *The Apostolic Fathers*.
26. Justin Martyr, *First Apology*, 44. Jurgens, *The Faith of the Early Fathers*, vol. 1.
27. Hermas, *Mandates*, 11.1. Lightfoot, *The Apostolic Fathers*.
28. Ibid., 10.2.
29. Justin Martyr, *First Apology*, 63. Richardson, *Early Christian Fathers*.
30. Hippolytus, *Commentary on Daniel*, 4.6. Jurgens, *The Faith of the Early Fathers*, vol. 1.
31. *Insight on the Scriptures*, 2:1019.
32. Justin Martyr, *First Apology*, 6. Richardson, *Early Christian Fathers*.
33. Ibid., 31.
34. Ibid., 32, 53.
35. Ibid., 32, 33, 39, 40, 41, 48.
36. Ibid., 38.
37. Ibid., 40.
38. Ibid., 44.
39. Ibid., 44, 61.
40. Ibid., 51, 59, 60.
41. Ibid., 63.
42. Ibid., 33.
43. Justin Martyr, *Dialogue with Trypho the Jew*, 61. Jurgens, *The Faith of the Early Fathers*, vol. 1.
44. Hippolytus, *Commentary on Daniel*, 4.6. Jurgens, *The Faith of the Early Fathers*, vol. 1.
45. Hippolytus, *The Little Labyrinth*, quoted in Eusebius Pamphilus, *Ecclesiastical Church*, 5.28.15. Jurgens, *The Faith of the Early Fathers*, vol. 1.
46. *At-One-Ment Between God and Man*, 53.

47. *Should You Believe in the Trinity?* 3, 4.
48. Gerald Bray, *Creeds, Councils, and Christ* (Leicester, England: Inter-Varsity Press, 1984), 107.
49. *Should You Believe in the Trinity?* 8.
50. Isaac Boyle, *A Historical View of the Council of Nice* (Philadelphia: J. B. Lippincott, 1879), 10-11.
51. Ibid., 13-14, 18-19.
52. Ibid., 47.
53. Ibid., 19.
54. Ibid.
55. *Letter of Eusebius Pamphilus to the Church of Caesarea,* ibid., 45
56. Boyle, *Council of Nice,* 28.
57. *Watchtower,* June 1, 1967, 338.
58. See Appendix.

5

The Soul, Death, and Resurrection

What is the nature of the human soul? According to Charles Russell, it is not what most Christians think.

> Not comprehending the meaning of the word soul, many feel at liberty to use it in a reckless manner, and hence they reverse the Scriptural statement and instead of speaking of man as *being* a soul, they speak of man as *having* a soul, which is a very different thought. . . . Thus the general idea of a soul is that it is wonderfully intelligent, possessed of wonderful powers, that it is indestructible, intangible, and incomprehensible. . . . But what is the

basis for such wild speculation? We answer, It is wholly unwarranted.[1]

Charles Russell reasoned that a human being consists of a physical body and an impersonal life power, the "spirit of life," which together constitute a soul—a living person, sustained by breathing. Man's soul or being, he taught, differs in no material way from that of the animals; his higher spiritual qualities are merely the product of a more capable mind than animals have.

> Those whose eyes of understanding begin to open to this subject . . . can readily see, from the foregoing, that every creature that possesses life-consciousness has, first of all, a body or organism; secondly, a spirit of life animating it; and thirdly, existence, being, soul, as a result.[2]

> Man as a soul is differentiated from the lower animals or souls by reason of his higher organism. . . . [I]t is in his mental and moral endowments rather than in physical form that man was created in the divine likeness.[3]

For Russell, this was true scriptural teaching, well known to the apostles, but lost in the apostasy of the church in the first several centuries.

Present Watchtower doctrine regarding the soul and the afterlife is virtually identical with that first taught by Russell. The Witnesses believe that all living beings, including animals, man, angels, and even God himself, are composed of two elements: a body (either physical or spiritual) and a life energy known as the spirit or life force.

As we have seen, the spirit is something different from our soul. The spirit is our life-force. This life-force is in each of the body cells of both humans and animals. It is sustained, or kept alive, by breathing. . . . At death the life-force in time leaves all the body cells and the body begins to decay.[4]

Man does not possess a soul as a separate entity; but rather, man *is* a soul. God and angels possess spirit bodies and a life force; man and animals, a physical body and a life force. Death results when the life force is separated from the body, which then decays; the life force or energy returns to God. This life force is an impersonal energy.

The life principle is one which pervades all creation just as does electricity. This principle of life pervades and is an essential element of all being, in tree, in fish, in fowl, in beast, in man, in angels, and in the fullest degree in God who is its source or fountain.[5]

One's life force is therefore devoid of any personal attributes and retains none of the characteristics of the individual after death:

It is clear that the "spirit" or life-force . . . is impersonal. . . . [T]he spirit, or life-force, that was active in man's body cells does not retain any of the characteristics of those cells. . . . Hence the personality of the dead individual is not perpetuated in the life force, or spirit.[6]

The Watchtower Society maintains that belief in a soul that survives death is a false Platonic idea introduced into the church by Greek converts. If this be the case, the leaders of the early church must have taught soul death, and the gradual amalgamation of the Platonic concept into church teaching should be evident over time. An examination of early Christian writings must once again provide our answers.

THE FATHERS AND THE NATURE OF THE SOUL

The term *soul* appears frequently in patristic literature, and, not unexpectedly, it is used with the same variety of meanings that it has in the Scriptures themselves. Barnabas, for example, uses the word repeatedly, at times describing the entire man, at times the inner man or heart, and often in quotes from the Septuagint (the Greek version of the Old Testament). The other postapostolic writers display similar patterns of use.

Those who learned at the feet of the apostles surely understood the nature of the soul and what happens to it at death, particularly since so many faced death itself at the hands of those who were eager to crush the faith. Such insight is indeed evident in narratives of martyrdom in the early church. Polycarp, the disciple of John, was martyred in 155 for refusing to deny Christ. He prayed at the moment of his death:

> I bless Thee, because Thou hast deemed me worthy this day and hour, to take my part among the number of the martyrs in the cup of thy Christ, for "resurrection to eternal life" of soul and body, in the immortality of the Holy Spirit; among whom may I be received in thy presence this day as a rich and acceptable sacrifice.[7]

Polycarp not only expressed faith in the coming resurrection of both body and soul, but rejoiced at the prospect of being in the presence of his Lord, along with the other martyrs, on "this day," the day of his death. His final words expressed the common hope of the early church. Death promised not a re-creation far in the future, but a prompt transport into the presence of the Lord himself.

This belief was demonstrated by others who suffered martyrdom for their love of Christ. The martyrs did not suffer joyfully because they hoped after a period of nonexistence to be re-created by God, but rather because they knew their painful death would usher them immediately into his presence—a prize well worth their frightful torments. Thus, Ignatius could exhort Christians on his way to death:

> Let me be fodder for wild beasts—that is how I can get to God. . . . I would rather that you fawn on the beasts so that they may be my tomb and no scrap of my body be left. Thus, when I have fallen asleep, I shall be a burden to no one. Then shall I be a real disciple of Jesus Christ when the world sees my body no more.[8]

Ignatius was motivated by the desire to be Christ's disciple after death, when the world could no longer see his body. Had he believed that his existence would cease at death, his statement would be meaningless.

Those who were persecuted and slaughtered for Christ were not alone in believing in an enduring, conscious afterlife, for such was the conviction of all faithful Christians and their leaders. Hermas, the contemporary of

Clement of Rome, expressed similar confidence in life after death. In the *Shepherd of Hermas* he speaks of apostolic preaching after death to those souls who had already fallen asleep:

> Because, saith he, these, the apostles and the teachers who preached the name of the Son of God, after they had fallen asleep in the power and faith of the Son of God, preached also to them that had fallen asleep before them, and themselves gave unto them the seal of their preaching.[9]

Those who argued in defense of the faith against pagan oppressors, pleading their case before philosophers and emperors, followed apostolic tradition when they wrote on the nature of the soul. Justin Martyr, for example, himself saved from the fruitless speculation of empty philosophy, declared:

> Look at the end of each of the former emperors, how they died the common death of all; and if this were merely a departure into unconsciousness, that would be a piece of luck for the wicked. But since consciousness continues for all who have lived, and eternal punishment awaits . . . all this should convince you that souls are still conscious after death. . . . we look forward to receiving again our own bodies, though they be dead and buried in the earth.[10]

Later patristic writers similarly demonstrated a belief in the continuation of conscious existence after death. For example, Irenaeus, the bishop of Lyons at the end of the second century, interpreted 1 Peter 3:19 as speaking of Christ's ministry to those in hades after his death.

> The Lord descended into the regions beneath the earth, announcing there the good news of His coming and the remission of sins conferred upon those who believe in Him.[11]

This explanation assumes that the spirit of Jesus survived death. Alert and conscious, he preached repentance and salvation to souls who had died before his time—souls that were themselves conscious and able in turn to respond to the gospel. Such an understanding is incompatible with any notion that the soul ceases to exist at death.

As time progressed, Christian theologians began discoursing specifically on the nature of the soul, the events surrounding death, and the coming resurrection. Athenagoras, the Athenian apologist, wrote one such dissertation, *Resurrection of the Dead*. Speaking of man's purpose and end, he says:

> It was for the sake of [men's] own life that [God] made them, and their life is not enkindled for a brief time, only to be completely snuffed out afterwards. . . . That, however, which was generated for the sake of its own life and existence . . . can never admit of any cause which would completely annihilate its existence. . . . Thus the soul exists and continues unchanged in the nature in which it was made.[12]

If this is merely the injection of Greek philosophy into Christian theology, it is a remarkable development, for *Res-*

113

urrection of the Dead was written less than one hundred years after the death of the apostles, within two generations. The harmony of Athenagoras with others who were disciples of the apostles, and the consistency of his concept of the soul with that expressed by other patristic authors, make Greek philosophy an implausible source for this understanding of the soul.

THE RESURRECTION OF THE DEAD

As the natural sleep, if sound, implies total unconsciousness, so with death, the figurative sleep; it is a period of absolute unconsciousness—more than that, it is a period of absolute non-existence, except as preserved in the Father's purpose and power. . . . The promise of resurrection is therefore a promise of relighting, a reenkindling of animal existence or soul.[13]

Watchtower resurrection theology has to harmonize two seemingly irreconcilable ideas: soul death, with cessation of existence, and the biblical promise of eternal life. The resulting formulation, not surprisingly, is rather complex. Furthermore, it has undergone considerable change over the years as major chronological milestones have been discarded or altered. An attempt to navigate these challenging waters is necessary, however, if Watchtower teachings are to be fairly compared with the faith of the post-apostolic church.

Jehovah's Witnesses understand the resurrection not as the restoration of an individual achieved by joining his soul to a resurrection body, but rather as the re-creation of

114

the individual from the life pattern contained in the memory of God. This fundamental belief, first taught by Russell, remains unaltered today.

> Resurrection is a restoration to life of the nonexistent dead. . . . It is an act of God dependent entirely on God's marvelous power through Christ and upon His memory of the dead. It is the reactivating of the life pattern of the creature, a transcription of which is on record with God, and is referred to as being in His memory.[14]

Woven into this re-creation theology is the class-based salvation taught by the Society. Briefly, Watchtower dogma since 1931 has declared that only an anointed class of 144,000 will attain heaven, and at their resurrection they will receive the spirit body that is needed to live in that realm. The vast majority of those who are saved will receive physical bodies and live in an earthly paradise. Those of the anointed class who died before Christ's parousia in 1914 are said to have been raised with spirit bodies like that of Christ in their own resurrection—one which indeed has already occurred, invisibly. Russell's view was somewhat different. He placed this resurrection in 1878, and he included in it all faithful Christians from Pentecost onward—a group he referred to as the "Church" or the "Bride of Christ." These would become partakers of the divine nature, as Christ had after his exaltation in heaven; in a very real sense, they would become gods.

> [The first resurrection] is not extended to the angels at all, but to the Son of Man and his "bride" to be chosen from among those whom he redeemed

115

with his own precious blood. . . . [Christ] has promised that his Church, his "bride", shall in resurrection be changed, by divine power, from human nature to the glory, honor, and immortality of the divine nature.[15]

Current Watchtower doctrine places this "first resurrection" in 1918, four years after the *parousia* (the invisible "presence" of Christ). While the exaltation to godhood has been deemphasized, in most other ways current Watchtower doctrine is indistinguishable from that of Russell.

So following the resurrection of Christ, the 144,000 are the next to be raised. . . . When does this take place? During his presence, the Bible says. . . . Christ's presence began in the year 1914. So the day for the first resurrection of faithful Christians to heaven has already come. . . . Of course, this first resurrection to heavenly life is unseen to human eyes.[16]

The next re-creation is known as the "resurrection to life." This is an earthly resurrection, in which the dead are raised to physical bodies. It will occur during the early part of the Millennium. Included in this event are faithful Witnesses who died before the time of Christ (that is, the Old Testament prophets and saints) and the "other sheep"— faithful Jehovah's Witnesses, not of the anointed class, who die before Armageddon.

Who are the righteous that are to be resurrected? These will include the faithful servants of God who lived before Jesus Christ came to earth. . . . They

116

did not hope to go to heaven, but hoped to live again on earth. Also among the righteous to be resurrected are the faithful servants of God who have died in recent years.[17]

The wicked who have sinned against the holy spirit will not be raised; their sentence is eternal nonexistence.

Persons who willfully do what is bad after knowing God's will may be sinning against the holy spirit. And God will not resurrect those who sin against his holy spirit.[18]

Lastly, a final resurrection will occur after Armageddon, to include

those persons whose hearts may have been wanting to do right, but who died without ever having an opportunity to hear of God's purposes or learn what he expects of men. Many of these have been decent people. They may have been sincere in their belief. But still they "practiced vile things."[19]

Resurrection and the Ante-Nicene Fathers

The Watchtower Society's complicated resurrection theology needs to be compared with the apostolic faith, for it bears no resemblance to historic Christian doctrine. If indeed the Jehovah's Witnesses have recaptured the apostolic teaching on the resurrection, then traditional doctrine must be seriously reconsidered. But if not, we must reject the Society's theology as nothing more than the product of human imagination. An examination of early Christian literature will help to settle this question.

Belief in the resurrection is widely evident in patristic literature. Many passages, however, speak only of the certainty of the event, without casting much light on its particulars. Other passages, however, present a clearer picture of early Christian doctrine. The ancient homily known as 2 *Clement* exhorts believers to live righteously with a view toward eternal life.

> Let us therefore practice righteousness that we may be saved unto the end. Blessed are they that obey these ordinances. Though they may endure affliction for a short time in the world, they will gather the immortal fruit of the resurrection. . . . The godly . . . shall live again in heaven with the fathers, and shall have rejoicing throughout a sorrowless eternity.[20]

The promise of eternal, blissful life in heaven after death was a strong incentive for holy living on a daily basis, as well as a comfort to those facing death. Death itself was perceived as a transition to eternal life in the presence of Christ.

> Obey the bishop and the presbytery without distraction of mind; breaking one bread, which is the medicine of immortality and the antidote that we should not die but live for ever in Jesus Christ.[21]

To understand and convey the doctrine of the resurrection to believers, the early church used apostolic tradition and teaching about the resurrection of Christ. As the firstfruits of the resurrection from the dead, the glorified Jesus was the reality upon which Christian resurrection theology was built. Ignatius, for example, expressed this conviction about Christ's bodily resurrection:

> For I know and believe that He was in the flesh even after the resurrection. . . . He said to them, "Lay hold and handle me, and see that I am not a demon without body." And straightway they touched Him, and they believed, being joined unto His flesh and His blood. Wherefore they also despised death, nay they were found superior to death. And after His resurrection He [both] ate with them and drank with them as one in the flesh, though spiritually He was united with the Father.[22]

For Ignatius, himself facing a cruel death, such words were not idle speculation, but living reality and comfort. Jesus Christ was risen, not as a spirit creature, but as flesh and blood. This conviction gave the martyrs great courage, for they were certain that they would see their Lord at death and be raised physically at his return. Polycarp expressed a similar hope as he prayed at the moment of his martyrdom.

> O Lord God Almighty, the Father of Thy beloved and blessed Son Jesus Christ . . . I bless Thee for that Thou hast granted me this day and hour, that I might receive a portion amongst the number of martyrs in the cup of [Thy] Christ unto the resurrection of eternal life, both of soul and of body, in the incorruptibility of the Holy Spirit. May I be received among these in Thy presence this day.[23]

119

As the church grew, literary attacks from pagan philosophers began to appear. In response, Christian apologetic literature began to discuss the major beliefs of Christianity, attempting to bring pagans to a deeper and more accurate understanding of the faith. Athenagoras, one of the most eloquent of the Apologists, wrote specifically on the topic of the resurrection:

> Among the other changes of age, appearance and size, is the resurrection. For the resurrection is a species of change, the last of all, and a change for the better. . . . If every example of human nature is made up jointly of an immortal soul and the body with which it is united at creation, and if God has decreed such an origin, . . . it is absolutely necessary, since one living being [is] formed of the two, experiencing whatever the soul experiences and whatever the body experiences, . . . that the whole series of these experiences must be referred to one and the same end.[24]

Athenagoras, in a well-developed theology of soul, life, and death, here maintains that human life, having been created by God through the union of body and immortal soul, must by its very nature be consummated in the resurrection. To end otherwise would contradict God's purpose in creating life in this fashion.

Justin Martyr also argued for the reality of the resurrection. Contrary to any assertion that the early church derived its doctrine of the resurrection from Greek philosophy, Justin countered pagan philosophical skepticism about life after death and the reuniting of soul and body in resurrection.

In the same way unbelief prevails about the resurrection of the dead because you have never seen an instance of it. But as you at first would not have believed that from a little drop [of human seed] such beings [as men] could develop, yet you see it happening, so consider that it is possible for human bodies, dissolved and scattered in the earth like seeds, to rise again in due time by God's decree and be clothed with incorruption.[25]

Patristic resurrection theology was not highly developed, and some differing concepts arose during the first several centuries. Hippolytus, for example, believed that God would renew the body that had died, as a seed germinates to form new growth. Such concepts, while somewhat peculiar, are nevertheless in harmony with the fundamental belief in the reunion of a living soul with a physical body.

We believe, therefore, that the body too is resurrected. . . . The earth receives its remains and preserves them; and they become like seed, wrapped up in the richer part of the earth, to spring up and bloom. . . . [S]o also to every body its own soul will be returned. . . . The unrighteous, however, will receive their bodies unchanged, neither freed from suffering and disease, nor glorified, but in those ills in which they died; and whatever they were before they were raised to life and reunited, and however they lived in faithlessness, according to that shall they be faithfully judged.[26]

Equally apparent from this passage is the conviction that the wicked would be raised, along with the righteous, to suffer judgment. There is no mention of the eternal destruction and nonexistence of the wicked, as taught by the Watchtower Society, in this or any other patristic work.

Hippolytus also provides us with a valuable glimpse into the tradition and worship of the church in the second century. In his *Apostolic Tradition*, he recounts the fundamental beliefs of the Christian faith and depicts its liturgical life in considerable detail. Describing the liturgy for baptizing new converts, he says:

> When the one being baptized goes down into the water, the one baptizing him shall put his hand on him. . . . And again he shall say: "Do you believe in the Holy Spirit and the holy Church and the resurrection of the flesh?" The one being baptized then says: "I believe."[27]

> You have already been instructed about the resurrection of the flesh and all else that is taught in the Scriptures.[28]

The second-century church, basing its practice on long-established apostolic tradition, required its initiates to confirm their faith in a resurrection of the flesh—not a resurrection to spirit bodies or a re-creation of physical ones, as Watchtower literature would have us believe.

The doctrine of the resurrection, like other doctrines, is not discussed in great detail in postapostolic Christian literature. What indications of early Christian doctrine we do have, however, are harmonious in virtually every respect with orthodox Christian teaching. The silence about a first, invisible resurrection to spirit bodies, a paradise on earth, an impersonal life force, and the eternal nonexistence of the wicked, is telling. When viewed in conjunction with the belief in an immortal soul that survives death, the patristic position on the resurrection bears no resemblance to Watchtower theology—and indeed condemns it as the fabrication of an imaginative nineteenth-century "pastor" and his followers.

HELL AND ETERNAL PUNISHMENT

The Watchtower Society has no sympathy for the traditional Christian doctrine of the eternal damnation of the wicked.

> We have seen clearly that the penalty or sentence against mankind was not eternal torture, but as plainly and distinctly stated by the Creator to Adam, it was death. . . . [I]t requires no particular ability of mind to discern that an eternity of torture for Father Adam would not have been a just penalty for his partaking of the forbidden fruit. . . . [M]uch more, it would not have been just to have permitted such a sentence of eternal torture to be entailed on the countless millions of Adam's posterity. . . . Our Lord did not go to everlasting torment, hence we have this indisputable testimony that everlasting torment is not the wages of sin prescribed by the great Judge, but merely a delusion, foisted upon mankind by the great Adversary, and those whom he has deluded.[29]

Apart from the deity of Jesus Christ, and the related doctrine of the Trinity, there is no Christian doctrine that has come under greater attack than that of the unceasing torment of recalcitrant sinners after death. But perhaps such assaults are warranted—surely a religion worshiping a God of love must have strayed into error when formulating such a heinous end for mankind. This was the light that initiated Charles Russell's search for biblical truth among the apostate doctrines of Christendom. His antipathy to the doctrine of eternal punishment remained untempered throughout his life, and it has been carried on without alteration to this day by the Society that he founded.

> Is hell hot, then? Not according to the Bible. Indeed, the Hebrew and Greek words translated in some Bibles as "hell" merely designate the common grave of dead humans. It is not a hot place of torment. It is, rather, a place of rest, from which the dead will come forth in the resurrection.[30]

> We have already noted that "the lake of fire and sulfur" could not be a literal place of torment. . . . [W]e read that death itself, along with Hades, is cast into this same lake of fire and sulfur. Surely, death and Hades cannot suffer pain! . . . "And they will be tormented day and night forever." . . . [I]t is not logical to say that symbols . . . could suffer torture in a literal way. Hence, we have no reason to believe that Satan will be suffering for all eternity. He is to be annihilated.[31]

The Society maintains that the early Church had no notion of eternal punishment. This doctrine supposedly resulted, as did so many other doctrines of Christendom,

from the great "falling away" of the first two centuries. The
Watchtower says:

> When did professed Christians adopt the belief in
> such an afterlife? Certainly not during the time of
> Jesus and his apostles. . . . The [apocryphal] *Apoc-
> alypse of Peter* . . . was the first Christian work to
> describe the punishment and tortures of sinners in
> hell. In fact it appears that among the early church
> fathers, there was much disagreement over hell.[32]

To test this assertion, a careful examination of early
Christian literature is warranted. Convincing evidence of
a pagan or speculative origin for the doctrine of hell would
certainly mandate a reexamination of its scriptural validity.

THE ANTE-NICENE WRITERS AND ETERNAL PUNISHMENT

The concept of eternal punishment is mentioned with
surprising frequency in early Christian literature. Indeed
there are few postapostolic writers who do not allude to
the fate of the wicked in at least one of their works. In
some instances these references are consistent with either
the annihilation of the wicked or their conscious punishment. Barnabas, for example, writing shortly after the destruction of Jerusalem, does not elaborate when he says of
the wicked:

> But the way of the Black One is crooked and full
> of a curse. For it is a way of eternal death with pun-

ishment in wherein are the things that destroy men's souls.[33]

For he that doeth these things shall be glorified in the kingdom of God; whereas he that chooses their opposites shall perish together with his works. . . . The day is at hand, in which everything shall be destroyed together with the Evil One.[34]

Other early writers give a more definite picture of the fate of unrepentant sinners. Clement, the bishop of Rome at the close of the first century, draws a parallel between the destruction of Sodom and the judgment coming at Christ's return.

Lot was saved from Sodom, when the whole countryside was condemned to fire and brimstone. In that way the Master made it clear that He does not forsake those who put their hope in Him, but delivers to punishment and torment those who turn away from him.[35]

While at first a parallel might be drawn between the destruction of Sodom and annihilation, Clement's reference to "torment" negates any such interpretation. Any notion that he might be speaking about eternal nonexistence is further undermined when he alludes to the fate of Korah, Dathan, and Abiram (Num. 16:23-33) while exhorting Christians to avoid hardheartedness.

It is better for a man to confess of his sins than to harden his heart in the way those rebels against God's servant Moses hardened theirs. The verdict against them was made very plain. For "they went down to Hades alive," and "Death will be their shepherd."[36]

Clement's emphasis on their descent *alive* to hades, with Death as their shepherd, precludes any possibility that he is merely using symbolic language. Nonexistent beings do not need shepherds.

The threat of eternal punishment was frequently used to exhort Christians to pursue a life of righteousness. While such a message might seem to deny the eternal security of the believer, it nevertheless demonstrates a firm conviction that a conscious condition of torment awaits the wicked after death. The homily known as 2 *Clement* illustrates this form of teaching in the early second century.

> For, if we do the will of Christ, we shall find rest; but if otherwise, then nothing shall deliver us from eternal punishment, if we should disobey his commandments.[37]

> For this cause is a man unable to attain happiness, seeing that they call in the fears of men, preferring rather the enjoyment which is here than the promise which is to come. For they know not how great a torment the enjoyment which is here bringeth, and what delight the promise which is to come bringeth.[38]

While the reference to "eternal punishment" by itself might suggest annihilation, the parallel drawn between the conscious "promise which is to come" (heaven) and the "torment" of the wicked surely implies that the torment in view is likewise conscious and eternal. The assertion that only a destruction to nonexistence is meant cannot be substantiated, for the homilist says,

> But the righteous, having done good and endured torments and hated the pleasures of the soul, when they shall behold them that have done amiss and denied Jesus by their words or by their deeds, how that they are punished with grievous torments in unquenchable fire, shall give glory to God.[39]

Such language is incompatible with any theology of soul death.

The martyrs, anticipating blissful life in the presence of the Lord at death, were equally convinced of the destiny of those who denied or blasphemed Christ. Indeed, the fear of eternal torment provided further motivation to face and endure the frightful agony of martyrdom. The fire of the pagan tormenter was brief; the eternal fire reserved for traitors to Christ was equally real, but far more frightening.

> And again [the proconsul said] to him, "I shall have you consumed with fire, if you despise the wild beasts, unless you change your mind." But Polycarp said: "The fire you threaten burns but an hour and is quenched after a little; for you do not know of the fire of the coming judgment and everlasting punishment that is laid up for the impious."[40]

> And giving themselves over to the grace of Christ, they despised the tortures of this world, purchasing for themselves in the space of one hour the life

eternal. To them the fire of their inhuman tortures was cold, for they set before their eyes escape from the fire that is everlasting and never quenched.[41]

Ignatius, another great martyr of the early church, understood as well the fate of those who opposed the faith—not a mere cessation of being, but the just punishment of an eternity in unquenchable fire.

If then they which do these things after the flesh are put to death, how much more if a man through evil doctrine corrupts the faith of God for which Jesus Christ was crucified. Such a man, having defiled himself, shall go into the unquenchable fire; and in like manner also shall he that hearkeneth unto him.[42]

The apologists who defended the faith before pagan philosophers and rulers often cited the great courage of the martyrs as evidence for the certainty of life after death—a blessed life for those committed to righteousness, but a fearful one for the unbeliever. In spite of the power of this testimony, they realized that this reality could not be perceived without repentance and a proper relationship with God. The author of the *Epistle to Diognetus*, pleading with his pagan audience in the hope of removing their spiritual blindness, says:

[When you become an imitator of God], then you will condemn the fraud and error of the world, once you really understand the true life in heaven, once you look down on the apparent death here be-

low, once you fear the real death kept for those who
are condemned to the eternal fire, which will punish those who are handed over to it. Then you will
admire those who for righteousness' sake endure
the transitory fire. . . . when you learn about that
other fire.[43]

The writer dismisses as well the foolishness of
philosophers who believe that God is but one of the elements, and he speaks clearly of their fate.

Or dost thou accept the empty and nonsensical
statements of those pretentious philosophers: of
whom some said that God was fire (they call that
God, to which they themselves shall go)?[44]

Justin Martyr, writing in the first half of the second
century, was unambiguous in declaring the existence of
hell for the wicked. His pre-Christian background as a pagan philosopher might lend credence to arguments that his
doctrine of hell was simply imported from his earlier convictions. Justin did indeed believe that the great philosophers had been given a seed of truth by God, and he often pointed out areas where their teaching contained elements of truth. This style of evangelistic writing was no
doubt intended to make Christianity more accessible to the
intellectual Greek. Justin did not equivocate, however, in
pointing out the foolishness of pagan philosophies where
they opposed the truth he had discovered in Christ, which
he had learned from disciples of the apostles. He specifically denied that Christianity had borrowed these ideas
from the pagans, despite the apparent similarity of teachings about life after death.

When we say that all things have been ordered and made by God we appear to offer the teaching of Plato—in speaking of a coming destruction by fire, that of the Stoics; in declaring that the souls of the unrighteous will be punished after death, still remaining in conscious existence, and those of the virtuous, delivered from punishments, will enjoy happiness, we seem to agree with various poets and philosophers.[45]

The source of this doctrine was not the philosophers themselves, however, despite any appearance of similarity;—rather, it was Christ. Justin believed that the philosophers, when they approximated the truth of the gospel, had derived their insights from God's own prophets.

It is this, in brief, that we look for, and have learned from Christ, and teach. Plato similarly said that Rhadamanthus and Minos would punish the wicked who came before them. We say that this is what will happen, but at the hands of Christ—and to the same bodies, reunited with their souls, and destined for eternal punishment.[46]

. . . everything that philosophers and poets said about the immortality of the soul, punishments after death, contemplation of heavenly things, and teachings of that kind—they took hints from the prophets and so were able to understand these things and expounded them.[47]

Justin's teaching, which he claimed to be that of Christ and the church, portrayed a conscious, eternal tor-

ment for the wicked, the consequence of righteous judgment by a just God. His purpose was not to generate fear
and hopelessness, but rather to motivate his listeners by
reason to repent, to turn from foolish idols and demon
worship to the salvation offered by a merciful God.

> We are . . . convinced . . . that everyone goes to eter-
> nal punishment or salvation in accordance with the
> character of his actions. If all men knew this, no-
> body would choose vice even for a little time,
> knowing that he was on his way to eternal pun-
> ishment by fire; every man would follow the self-
> restrained and orderly path of virtue, so as to re-
> ceive the good things that come from God and
> avoid his punishments.[48]

> We believe . . . that every man will suffer in eter-
> nal fire in accordance with the quality of his ac-
> tions, and similarly will be required to give ac-
> count for the abilities which he has received from
> God.[49]

There was justice, he believed, in eternal punishment.
The demise of those whose lives manifested evil, with a
simple passage into nonexistence, would be a stroke of for-
tune for them.

> Look at the end of each of the former emperors,
> how they died the common death of all; and if this
> were merely a departure into unconsciousness, that
> would be a piece of luck for the wicked. But since
> consciousness continues for all who have lived, and
> eternal punishment awaits, do not fail to be con-

vinced and believe that these things are true. . . .
[S]ouls are still conscious after death.[50]

The justice of punishment for the wicked seemed
most fitting to Justin when applied to Satan, who as the
chief of evil spirits entices men to immorality.

> Among us the chief of the evil demons is called the
> serpent and Satan and the devil, as you can learn
> by examining our writings. Christ has foretold that
> he will be cast into fire with his host and the men
> who follow him, all to be punished for endless
> ages.[51]

> [Christ] shall come from the heavens in glory with
> His angelic host when He shall raise the bodies of
> all the men who ever lived. Then He will clothe the
> worthy in immortality; but the wicked, clothed in
> eternal sensibility, He will commit to the eternal
> fire, along with the evil demons.[52]

For Justin, the certainty of hell parallels the reward of
heaven—if there is eternal, conscious life in heaven for the
righteous, there must also be conscious punishment for
those who are enemies of God. Justin brings up the threat
of hell repeatedly in his writings to motivate his pagan audience to accept the salvation afforded by the gospel. Justin
would have rejected the Society's doctrine of death as lu-
dicrous and unbalanced—and, as the above citation
demonstrates, their notion of Christ's invisible return
would have received a similar verdict.

Theophilus, the seventh bishop of Antioch, a church
second in prominence only to Rome, gave a similar de-

scription of the fate of unrepentant sinners in his apology *To Autolycus*, written at the end of the second century.

> Give studious attention to the prophetic writings and they will lead you on a clearer path to escape the eternal punishments and to obtain the eternal good things of God. . . . To those who seek immortality by the patient exercise of good works, He will give everlasting life, joy, peace, rest, and all good things. . . . For the unbelievers and for the contemptuous . . . there will be wrath and indignation, tribulation and anguish. In the end, such men as these will be detained in everlasting fire.[53]

Irenaeus, generally regarded as the most important theologian of the second century, wrote his great five-volume treatise *Against Heresies* in about the year 180. Relating the teaching he had received from Polycarp and other disciples of the apostles, Irenaeus speaks of the judgment of Christ at the end of the age.

> The Church . . . received from the apostles . . . its faith . . . that [Christ] may make just judgment of them all; and that He may send the spiritual forces of wickedness, and the angels who transgressed and became apostates, and the impious, unjust, lawless and blasphemous among men, into everlasting fire.[54]

> For to whomever the Lord shall say, "Depart accursed ones, into the everlasting fire", they will be damned forever.[55]

Could this great theologian have been confused, reciting an ancient Babylonian myth rather than apostolic truth, as the Witnesses would maintain? Such an assertion about a man who had learned at the feet of a disciple of John is hardly plausible. In this matter, Irenaeus is in complete harmony with those who preceded him.

Later writers not only supported the certainty of conscious punishment for the unjust, but elaborated on its nature as well. Hippolytus, in his treatise *Against the Greeks*, written about 220, speaks of the judgment seat of Christ and the inevitable consequences for both the good and the evil.

> Standing before [Christ's] judgment, all of them, men, angels, and demons, crying out in one voice, shall say: "Just is your judgment!" . . . To those who have done well, everlasting enjoyment shall be given; while to the lovers of evil shall be given eternal punishment. The unquenchable and unending fire awaits these latter, and a certain fiery worm which does not die and which does not waste the body, but continually bursts forth from the body with unceasing pain. No sleep will give them rest; no night will soothe them; no death will deliver them from punishment; no appeal of interceding friends will profit them.[56]

This graphic description is incompatible with any belief in the annihilation of the wicked. Written by a respected church leader only two generations after the death of the apostles, it can hardly be dismissed as pure speculation, entirely removed from the teachings of the apostles themselves. While the details of eternal torment given by

135

Hippolytus may involve a degree of conjecture, his basic conviction about hell certainly reflects the teachings of the church from its beginning.

Tertullian, Clement of Alexandria, and Origen all depict the sufferings of evil men after death. Their accounts are in close harmony with those who came before, and they show no evidence of an evolution toward a more speculative Greek-Christian syncretism. Admittedly, Origen's doctrine of the soul was errant, and he was castigated for it by the church some centuries after his death. He also subscribed to universalism, claiming that after a time of punishment God in his mercy would spare even the wicked. But Origen believed in the continued existence of the soul after death and the punishment of evildoers in hell. In his work *Fundamental Doctrines*, he discusses what he believes to be the crucial doctrines of the Christian faith, passed down directly from the apostles.

> It ought to be known, however, that the holy Apostles, in preaching the faith of Christ, treated with the utmost clarity certain matters which they believed to be of absolute necessity to all believers, even to those who seemed somewhat dull in regard to the investigation of divine knowledge.[57]

Among those doctrines presented by the apostles with a clarity that even the "dull" could understand were the teachings about the soul and eternal punishment. Origen presents the final events in a familiar way, treating eternal reward for goodness and endless torment for evil in parallel fashion.

> Therefore and on this account it is most fitting that the soul, without waiting for the flesh, be punished

for what it did without the partnership of the flesh. And for pious and benevolent thoughts in which it shared not with the flesh, without the flesh it shall be refreshed.[58]

Now let us see what is meant by the threatening with eternal fire. . . . [E]very sinner kindles for himself the flame of his own fire and is not plunged into some fire which was kindled beforehand by someone else or which already existed before him. The food and fuel of this fire are our sins, which are called wood and hay and stubble by the Apostle Paul.[59]

Origen's belief in the fire of hell finds ample support in Christian tradition from the earliest times. As with many of the fathers, his depiction of hell's torments may not be correct. But the certainty of some state of torment after death cannot be questioned.

Sinful man has always scoffed at the idea that his rebellion against God has eternal consequences. Even in the contemporary church there is much reluctance to speak of hell, particularly in an evangelistic context. However, no such reticence existed among the teachers and apologists of an earlier age; rather, the certainty of eternal punishment was a cornerstone of their appeal to the pagan world. It may be argued, at least by the number of references, that hell was a dominant theme of the postapostolic period. In contrast, there is no direct reference to soul death or the re-creation–resurrection theology espoused by the Watchtower Society. What few ambiguous references exist about the nature of eternal punishment are completely overshadowed by the testimony of many that the unsaved face eternal torment in hell.

NOTES

1. Charles T. Russell, *Studies in the Scriptures*, vol. 5: *The At-One-Ment Between God and Man* (Brooklyn: International Bible Students Association, 1891), 320.
2. Ibid., 340.
3. Ibid., 326.
4. *You Can Live Forever in Paradise on Earth* (Brooklyn: Watchtower Bible and Tract Society of New York, 1982), 78.
5. *Watchtower*, April 1, 1981, 205.
6. *Insight on the Scriptures* (Brooklyn: Watchtower Bible and Tract Society of New York, 1988), 2:1025.
7. *Martyrdom of Polycarp*, 14. Cyril C. Richardson, *Early Christian Fathers* (New York: Macmillan, 1970).
8. Ignatius, *Romans*, 4. Richardson, *Early Christian Fathers*.
9. Hermas, *Similitudes*, 9.16. J. B. Lightfoot, *The Apostolic Fathers* (1891; reprint, Grand Rapids: Baker, 1956).
10. Justin Martyr, *First Apology*, 18. Richardson, *Early Christian Fathers*.
11. Irenaeus, *Against Heresies*, 4.27.2. William A. Jurgens, *The Faith of the Early Fathers*, vol. 1 (Collegeville, Minn. Liturgical Press, 1979).
12. Athenagoras, *Resurrection of the Dead*, 12. Jurgens, *The Faith of the Early Fathers*, vol. 1.
13. Russell, *At-One-Ment Between God and Man*, 343.
14. *Make Sure of All Things* (Brooklyn: Watchtower Bible and Tract Society, 1953), 311.
15. Russell, *At-One-Ment Between God and Man*, 394.
16. *You Can Live Forever in Paradise on Earth*, 173.
17. Ibid., 172.
18. Ibid., 171.
19. *From Paradise Lost to Paradise Regained* (Brooklyn: Watchtower Bible and Tract Society, 1958), 229.
20. *2 Clement*, 19. Lightfoot, *The Apostolic Fathers*.
21. Ignatius, *Ephesians*, 20. Lightfoot, *The Apostolic Fathers*.

22. Ignatius, *Smyrneans*, 3. Lightfoot, *The Apostolic Fathers*.
23. *Martyrdom of Polycarp*, 14. Lightfoot, *The Apostolic Fathers*.
24. Athenagoras, *Resurrection of the Dead*, 12. Jurgens, *The Faith of the Early Fathers*, vol. 1.
25. Justin Martyr, *First Apology*, 19. Richardson, *Early Christian Fathers*.
26. Hippolytus, *Against the Greeks*, 2. Jurgens, *The Faith of the Early Fathers*, vol. 1.
27. Hippolytus, *Apostolic Tradition*, 21. Jurgens, *The Faith of the Early Fathers*, vol. 1.
28. Ibid., 23.
29. Russell, *At-One-Ment Between God and Man*, 422, 441.
30. *Watchtower*, October 1, 1989, 7.
31. *Revelation* (Brooklyn: Watchtower Bible and Tract Society, 1988), 293-94.
32. *Watchtower*, October 1, 1989, 6.
33. *Barnabas*, 20. Lightfoot, *The Apostolic Fathers*.
34. Ibid., 21.
35. *1 Clement*, 11. Richardson, *Early Christian Fathers*.
36. Ibid., 51. Richardson, *Early Christian Fathers*.
37. *2 Clement*, 6. Lightfoot, *The Apostolic Fathers*.
38. Ibid., 10.
39. Ibid., 17.
40. *Martyrdom of Polycarp*, 11. Richardson, *Early Christian Fathers*.
41. Ibid., 2.
42. Ignatius, *Ephesians*, 16. Lightfoot, *The Apostolic Fathers*.
43. *Epistle to Diognetus*, 10. Richardson, *Early Christian Fathers*.
44. Ibid., 8
45. Justin Martyr, *First Apology*, 20. Richardson, *Early Christian Fathers*.
46. Ibid., 8.
47. Ibid., 44.
48. Ibid., 12.
49. Ibid., 17.
50. Ibid., 18.

51. Ibid., 28.
52. Ibid., 52.
53. Theophilus, *To Autolycus*, 1.14. Jurgens, *The Faith of the Early Fathers*, vol. 1.
54. Irenaeus, *Against Heresies*, 1.10.1. Richardson, *Early Christian Fathers*.
55. Ibid., 4.28.2. Jurgens, *The Faith of the Early Fathers*, vol. 1.
56. Hippolytus, *Against the Greeks*, 3. Jurgens, *The Faith of the Early Fathers*, vol. 1.
57. Origen, *Fundamental Doctrines*, 1.pref.3. Jurgens, *The Faith of the Early Fathers*, vol. 1.
58. Ibid., 1.pref.5.
59. Ibid., 2.10.3.

6

The Verdict

It is dangerous to build theology solely on the post-apostolic writings, and considerable caution is required for such an undertaking. It must be recognized that some postapostolic beliefs, particularly on minor issues, are difficult to substantiate scripturally. Such formulations, which were often the product of philosophical speculation, have ultimately been rejected by the church. This should come as no surprise, for several reasons. Although the Fathers used the Septuagint and the available New Testament writings extensively in teaching, evangelism, and exhortation, they did not direct much effort at comprehensive scriptural analysis and exegesis. It was not until Origen's monumental effort during the third century that anything approaching such a work was drafted, and his philosophical meandering seriously flawed even that great effort. Furthermore, the writers of the ante-Nicene period were not uniform in their intellectual gifts or academic background. Some, such as Hermas, produced long, ponderous works, which, although respected in their own time, ultimately failed to have any impact on the church's understanding of its faith. Many postapostolic works were not doctrinal treatises, but simply letters or homilies to discipline and build up the flock. It would be unreasonable to expect these works to bear the entire weight of apostolic teaching and subsequent doctrinal development. The principal value of postapostolic literature is rather that it documents Christian life and thought in the first few centuries. It is in this role that we may utilize it, not to *form* doctrines, but rather to *confirm* that teaching now declared to be biblical and apostolic is in fact biblical and apostolic.

Much skepticism exists today about the historical value of the Gospels and early Christian writings—a cynicism that does not extend to other historical writing of this period. Such a perspective no doubt arises from the potential impact of Christianity's teaching on one's own life. Enormous implications are inescapable once the conclusion is drawn that God intervened in human history in the person of Jesus Christ. Some would prefer to change history rather than change their minds.

For those who accept the evidence of history, honest scholarship dictates that careful attention be paid to the literary and cultural context of the writings of the church fathers. Every effort should be made to avoid approaching such a study with predetermined conclusions. Just as one can prove virtually anything by reading meaning into the

Bible, so can one twist early Christian literature to yield conclusions at variance with the truth.

I recognize that my own bias as someone within the orthodox Christian tradition can and does color my interpretation of this literature. I have sought to be objective, avoiding conclusions where evidence is weak or lacking. Anyone so inclined should read these works for himself and draw the appropriate conclusions. This body of literature is quite manageable in size, and it contains some beautifully written prose and elegantly crafted defenses of a new and growing religion. For these reasons alone, such an effort would be time well spent, apart from any benefit it might confer as an apologetic for contemporary Christian thought. Modern translations have made this literature readily accessible to all.

I believe it would be impossible for any honest student of the postapostolic era to construct a broad-based defense of the teachings advanced by the Watchtower Society. There is an absolute dearth of support in patristic literature for the Society's portrait of Jehovah's Kingdom. If we reasonably assume that the church fathers touched upon the elements of their faith that they judged to be important, their cumulative silence on key Witness teachings is devastating. There is no evidence that the early church understood itself to be God's organization on earth. There is no knowledge of two categories of salvation or of a paradise on earth. Hell was a frightening reality, threatening the pagan and motivating the believer to keep the faith. Martyrs died victoriously, confident of immediate conscious bliss in the presence of their Lord. And above all, in the church fathers we see Jesus—fully God and fully man, bodily risen, and coming again in full, visible glory. One can only conclude that the teachings of the Jehovah's Witnesses represent a new religious tradition rather than a restoration of the true gospel lost by an apostate church.

THE ORIGINS OF WATCHTOWER THEOLOGY

The peculiar doctrines of the Jehovah's Witnesses can be traced back to deviant forms of Christianity in preceding centuries—"there is nothing new under the sun" (Eccl. 1:9). While there is no single heretical movement in the first few centuries that entirely resembles Russellism, one can discern in various unorthodox movements the building blocks of modern-day Watchtower teaching.

From the earliest days of apostolic evangelism there were those who, while nominally acknowledging Jesus as the Messiah, rejected the salvation that he freely provided by grace through faith. The Ebionites, a Jewish-Christian sect that arose from the legalistic Jewish opposition to Paul, was one such group. They foreshadowed the Watchtower Society by emphasizing obedience to the law and hoping by their asceticism to be worthy of God's acceptance. Contemporary Jehovah's Witnesses continue to struggle under the unbearably heavy burden of adhering not only to every dictate of the law of Jehovah, but to the ever-changing "truth" promulgated by the organization to which they have submitted.

The Jehovah's Witnesses have occasionally been charged with being a Gnostic religion. This accusation is not entirely accurate. Watchtower theology contains little of Gnosticism's primary dogmas, such as its dualistic worldview, according to which flesh is evil and spirit is inherently good. Yet there are numerous Witness beliefs with which the Gnostics would have been comfortable. Their docetic view of Christ's resurrection, while not grounded in the conviction that the flesh is evil, nevertheless is quite similar to some Gnostic speculation. By making Jesus a second, subordinate god in order to avoid the implications of his full deity, they hark back to the angelic intermediaries that the Gnostics placed between the unknowable holy God and the corrupt creation. The greatest similarity between the Witnesses and the Gnostics, however, is that their relationship to God is predicated on special knowledge.

The Gnostics separated themselves from the lost masses of humanity by virtue of their higher knowledge of God and the spiritual realm. This explains their name, for the Greek word *gnosis* means "knowledge." Knowledge—exclusive, privileged knowledge—is likewise at the heart of the Watchtower gospel.

> This, then, is our Lord's answer to the question of the disciples. . . . There will be no sign for the worldly masses; they will not know of my presence and the new dispensational changes. Only a few will know, and they will be taught of God before there is any sign which the worldly could discern.[1]

> It is to express . . . this "blessedness" and fuller unfolding of the divine plan, now due to be understood by all the "holy people" now living, [that] the *Scripture Studies* series is being published. None but the "holy people" will understand it.[2]

> What does God require of those who will reside forever upon his Paradise earth? . . . Jesus Christ

145

> identified a first requirement when he said in
> prayer to his Father: "This means everlasting life,
> their *taking in knowledge* of you, the only true God."
> . . . Knowledge of God and Jesus Christ includes
> knowledge of God's purposes regarding the earth
> and of Christ's role as earth's new King. Will you
> take in such knowledge by studying the Bible?[3]

For the Christian, knowledge of God is important. But far more important than intellectual comprehension is the personal, spiritual intimacy that comes about only by vigorously pursuing holy living under the guidance and empowerment of the Spirit, indwelling the heart of the believer. The distance from the mind to the heart is long indeed for those whose spirit has not been made alive by regeneration. The Watchtower gospel emphasizes cerebral comprehension of Jehovah, garnered through the filter of the Society's literature—an emphasis so dominant that they have brought their *New World Translation* into conformity with it. Unfortunately, higher knowledge cannot save man from the depravity of sin.

The closest historical antecedent for the Jehovah's Witnesses is found in Arianism. Arius taught that Christ was a lesser god, a position he holds today in Watchtower teaching. The Arian arguments were reasonable and widely popular, seemingly backed by Scripture verses and the support of ancient traditions. Arius himself was a charismatic leader and he cleverly set his theological ideas to melodies.

The Watchtower Christology is virtually indistinguishable from Arianism. The scriptural proof texts used in the *Watchtower* are identical to those used by Arius, and their exegesis shows a striking similarity to arguments rejected at Nicaea in the fourth century. As in the case of Gnosticism, however, the parallels are limited. There is silence from Arius on Jehovah's kingdom, the nature of the soul, the invisible return of Christ, and the afterlife. He denied the deity of the Spirit, but believed him to be a personal, though created, being. Russell was aware of the teachings of Arianism and applauded them, but he used the movement more for historical confirmation than as a doctrinal wellspring. The contemporary Society denies its roots in Arianism, while applauding its doctrine of Christ.

Contemporary Jehovah's Witnesses and the organization that leads them exhibit some ambivalence about their own roots in the teachings of Charles Russell. There are frequent references to Russell and his writings in the *Watchtower,* and he is spoken of with some reverence as a serious Bible student and a key instrument of Jehovah's holy spirit in restoring true religion. Nonetheless, Witnesses deny heatedly that Russell was the founder of their religion, and they view the label "Russellites" as one of contempt. This ambivalence has its roots in the historical transition of their movement from a personal cult of Russell to an organization led by Rutherford and his successors. After the abject failure of Russell's Armageddon prophecies, he and his followers were widely derided and a new identity was needed. Their transformation was completed in the early 1930s when the name Jehovah's Witnesses was adopted, but there remains a sensitivity even today among Witnesses about their Russellite origins. Any objective comparison of the doctrines of the modern Society with those of Russell leaves no doubt about their origin, however. Apart from the changes in chronology mandated by failed predictions, there is little to differentiate between them—even their language is identical in many

147

places. We may therefore judge the Society reliably by assessing the teachings of its founder, as well as those currently published in the *Watchtower*.

Despite ongoing efforts by the Watchtower Society to establish historical roots in the early church by using the postapostolic writings, it is clear that early Christian literature provides the Witnesses with no support for their dogmas. While we may commend the Witnesses for their zeal for the Bible, they are pursuing and propagating an illusion. Theirs is a faith that bears no resemblance to that established by Christ and his apostles, a faith foreign as well to the church that they established. Notwithstanding the Witnesses' frequent allegations about the apostasy of orthodox Christianity, it is they who need to defend themselves against this charge in light of the historical record.

Since individual Jehovah's Witnesses are discouraged from doing independent research apart from the *Watchtower* literature, there is little likelihood that they will investigate early Christian literature on their own initiative, as they have little reason to suspect that the Society has mislead them. Therefore, it behooves us as Christians to raise these issues in our interactions with them. We must plant seeds of uncertainty, which the Holy Spirit, in his own time and manner, can exploit. The wisdom of Proverbs exhorts us:

> Rescue those being led away to death; hold back those staggering toward slaughter. If you say, "But we knew nothing about this," does not he who weighs the heart perceive it? Does not he who guards your life know it? Will he not repay each person according to what he has done? (Prov. 24:11-12)

Early Christian apologists went to great lengths to defend their faith and lead to Christ those who had been waylaid by false religions and heretical doctrines. We owe the Witnesses no less an effort if we are to carry out our Savior's desire to seek and save the lost.

NOTES

1. Charles T. Russell, *Studies in the Scriptures,* vol. 2: *The Time Is at Hand* (Brooklyn: International Bible Students Association, 1889), 161, 163.
2. Charles T. Russell, *Studies in the Scriptures,* vol 3: *Thy Kingdom Come* (Brooklyn: International Bible Students Association, 1891), 88.
3. *Watchtower,* February 15, 1983, 12.

Appendix

The Watchtower Society booklet *Should You Believe in the Trinity?*[1] represents the most substantive recent attempt by the Witnesses to undermine orthodox Christian belief in the nature of the Godhead. In this work the Society attempts to refute the historical basis for the doctrine of the Trinity by citing references from the early church fathers. The section on the church fathers appears on page 7 of the booklet (Fig. 1).

None of the sources quoted in *Should You Believe in the Trinity?* are footnoted. To determine the source and accuracy of their assertions about the ante-Niceaen fathers, I wrote the Watchtower Society, requesting specific references for each of the church fathers cited. In response I received a letter and photocopies of selected pages from a single book, Alvan Lamson's *The Church of the First Three Centuries*[2] (Figs. 2 and 3). No other materials or direct references to the works of the Fathers themselves were enclosed.

Comparing the *Trinity* booklet with the Lamson photocopies and the writings of the Fathers reveals a number of discrepancies. The booklet states, for example, "Justin Martyr, who died about 165 C.E., called the prehuman Jesus a created angel. . . ." As we have shown (see pp. 49–51), Justin did refer to Christ as "Angel," but by this he meant the Angel of the Lord, whom he identified with the Lord God himself. Justin never said that Jesus was created. No substantiation for this statement appears in Lamson's book either, and hence we must conclude that this statement is without supporting evidence and merely reflects the opinion and theology of the Watchtower Society. The *Trinity* booklet goes on to say, "He [Justin] said that Jesus was inferior to God. . . ." This, however, is the conclusion of Lamson, not Justin (Fig. 4).

Similarly, the brochure says "Irenaeus, who died about 200 C.E., said that the prehuman Jesus had a separate existence from God and was inferior to him." This, once again, is a statement of Lamson's opinion rather than a paraphrase of any statement by Ireneaus (Fig. 5). Speaking of Clement, the booklet says, "Clement of Alexandria, who died about 215 C.E., called Jesus in his prehuman existence 'a creature'. . . ." Again, even Lamson does not say this—he is instead quoting Photius, a ninth-century critic of Clement (Fig. 6).

It is important to keep in mind that my request to the Society was very specific, asking for exact citations from the church fathers to support their claims in the *Trinity* booklet. In response, they sent photocopies of selected pages from a single secondary source and actually attributed to the church fathers the opinions of the author of that source, Alvan Lamson. It seems reasonable to conclude that the doctrines put forth in *Should You Believe in the Trinity?* were not based on an objective review of the early Christian writers.

NOTES

1. *Should You Believe in the Trinity?* (Brooklyn, N.Y.: Watchtower Bible and Tract Society, 1989).
2. *The Church of the First Three Centuries* (Riverside, Cambridge: H. O. Houghton & Co., 1869).

What the Ante-Nicene Fathers Taught

THE ante-Nicene Fathers were acknowledged to have been leading religious teachers in the early centuries after Christ's birth. What they taught is of interest.

Justin Martyr, who died about 165 C.E., called the prehuman Jesus a created angel who is "other than the God who made all things." He said that Jesus was inferior to God and "never did anything except what the Creator . . . willed him to do and say."

Irenaeus, who died about 200 C.E., said that the prehuman Jesus had a separate existence from God and was inferior to him. He showed that Jesus is not equal to the "One true and only God," who is "supreme over all, and besides whom there is no other."

Clement of Alexandria, who died about 215 C.E., called Jesus in his prehuman existence "a creature" but called God "the uncreated and imperishable and only true God." He said that the Son "is next to the only omnipotent Father" but not equal to him.

Tertullian, who died about 230 C.E., taught the supremacy of God. He observed: "The Father is different from the Son (another), as he is greater; as he who begets is different from him who is begotten; he who sends, different from him who is sent." He also said: "There was a time when the Son was not. . . . Before all things, God was alone."

Hippolytus, who died about 235 C.E., said that God is "the one God, the first and the only One, the Maker and Lord of all," who "had nothing co-eval [of equal age] with him . . . But he was One, alone by himself; who, willing it, called into being what had no being before," such as the created prehuman Jesus.

Origen, who died about 250 C.E., said that "the Father and Son are two substances . . . two things as to their essence," and that "compared with the Father, [the Son] is a very small light."

Summing up the historical evidence, Alvan Lamson says in *The Church of the First Three Centuries:* "The modern popular doctrine of the Trinity . . . derives no support from the language of Justin [Martyr]: and this observation may be extended to all the ante-Nicene Fathers; that is, to all Christian writers for three centuries after the birth of Christ. It is true, they speak of the Father, Son, and . . . holy Spirit, but not as co-equal, not as one numerical essence, not as Three in One, in any sense now admitted by Trinitarians. The very reverse is the fact."

Thus, the testimony of the Bible and of history makes clear that the Trinity was unknown throughout Biblical times and for several centuries thereafter.

"There is no evidence that any sacred writer even suspected the existence of a [Trinity] within the Godhead."—*The Triune God*

Fig. 1. *Should You Believe in the Trinity?*, p. 7.

WATCHTOWER
BIBLE AND TRACT SOCIETY OF NEW YORK, INC.

CABLE WATCHTOWER

WRITING DEPARTMENT
25 COLUMBIA HEIGHTS, BROOKLYN, NEW YORK 11201, U.S.A.

PHONE (718) 625-3600

EX:ESE   December 13, 1989

Mr Robert U Finnerty
811 N Stadium Way
Tacoma, WA 98403

Dear Mr. Finnerty:

We are just now able to respond to your letter received
November 1, 1989, in which you ask for references to the quotation from some of the Ante-Nicene Fathers as quoted in the
brochure <u>Should You Believe in the Trinity?</u>

In harmony with your request, we are sending you the enclosed information and trust that you will find this to be not
only interesting, but beneficial.

Along with our letter and the enclosed information, we would
like to take the occasion to send an expression of our best
wishes.

Sincerely,

Watchtower B.+T. Society
OF NEW YORK, INC.

Enclosure

Fig. 2. Letter from the Watchtower Society

THE CHURCH

OF THE

FIRST THREE CENTURIES:

OR,

NOTICES OF THE LIVES AND OPINIONS OF THE EARLY FATHERS,

WITH SPECIAL REFERENCE TO

THE DOCTRINE OF THE TRINITY;

ILLUSTRATING ITS

LATE ORIGIN AND GRADUAL FORMATION.

BY

ALVAN LAMSON, D.D.

SECOND EDITION, REVISED AND ENLARGED.

BOSTON:
HORACE B. FULLER.
14 BROMFIELD STREET.
1869.

Fig. 3. Title page of Lamson's book

of the universe is represented as raising him from the earth, and placing him at his right hand.* He expressed reliance on God, says Justin, for support and safety; nor, he continues, does he profess to do anything of his own will or power. He refused to be called "good"; replying, "One is good, — my Father, who is in heaven." † Again: Justin speaks of him in the following terms: "Who, *since he is the first-begotten Logos of God, is God";* ‡ that is, he is God by virtue of his birth: in other words, he derived a divine nature from God, just as we derive a human nature from human parents. This was what Justin and others meant when they spoke of the divinity of Christ.

Justin uses another class of expressions, which show that the supremacy of the Father was still preserved in his time. He represents Christians as approaching the Father *through* the Son. *Through* him, he says, they offered thanks and prayers to God; as we do always beseech God, *through* Jesus Christ, to preserve us from the power of demons. § In the account he gives of the celebration of the Supper, he observes that the person presiding "offers up praise and glory to the Father of the universe, *through* the name of the Son and the Holy Spirit." ‖ Again: "In all our oblations we bless the Maker of the universe, *through* his Son Jesus Christ, and through the Holy Spirit." ¶ From these passages, as well as from the whole strain of Justin's writings, it is evident that the Son was not regarded in his time as an object of direct address in prayer. No expression occurs, in any part of his works, which affords the slightest ground for the supposition, that supreme religious homage was ever rendered him, or that his name was ever directly invoked in the devotions of Christians. Prayer was as yet uniformly offered to God *through* the Son, according to the models left in the Scriptures.

We might multiply proofs; but it is unnecessary. We have adduced evidence sufficient, and more than sufficient, we conceive, to demonstrate beyond the possibility of cavil, that Justin regarded the Son as distinct from God, and inferior to him:

* *Dial.*, p. 129; Otto, c. 82.
‡ *Apol.* I., p. 81; Otto, c. 68.
‖ *Apol.* I., p. 82; Otto, c. 65.
† *Dial.*, p. 196; Otto, c. 101.
§ *Dial.*, p. 128; Otto, c. 80.
¶ *Apol.* I., p. 88; Otto, c. 67.

Fig. 4. Lamson, p. 73.

preceding Fathers already named, he agreed in assigning to
the Son a separate existence, making him inferior to the
Father; but the mode of his generation he would not discuss,
deeming it inexplicable. In his antagonism to the Gnostic
doctrine of emanations, he was led to connect with the Son
the terms "always" and "eternal"; it is difficult to define in
what sense. He wants clearness, and his notions seem not to
have been well defined even to himself. "Who," he asks,
with the prophet, "can declare his generation? No one.
No one knows it; not Valentinus, not Marcion, neither Satur-
ninus, nor Basilides, nor angels, nor archangels, nor princes,
nor powers, none but the Father who begat, and the Son who
was begotten." He is very careful, however, on all occasions
to distinguish the Son from the "One true and only God,"
who is "supreme over all, and besides whom there is no
other." Take two or three passages as specimens. "The
Father is above all, and is himself the head of Christ." *
"John preached one God supreme over all, and one only-be-
gotten Son Jesus Christ."† "The Church dispersed throughout all the world has received from the Apostles and their
disciples this belief — in one God the Father, supreme over
all . . . . and in one Jesus Christ . . . . and in the Holy Spirit,
that through the prophets preached the dispensations," etc.‡
We could fill pages with similar passages. No language could
more clearly and positively assert the supremacy of the Father.

The Father sends, the Son is sent; the Father commands,
the Son executes, ministering to his will. The Father grants,
the Son receives power and dominion. The Father *gives* him
the "heritage of the nations," and "subjects all his enemies
to him." § These and similar expressions which form his current phraseology, — which are interwoven, in fact, with the
texture of his whole work against heresies, — could not have
been employed by one who conceived of the Son as numerically
the same being with the Father, or as in any sense his equal.

Again : he quotes the words of the Saviour (Mark xiii. 32) :

* *Contra Hær.*, lib. v. c. 18, § 2.
† *Ibid.*, lib. i. c. 9, § 2.
‡ *Ibid.*, lib. i. c. 10, § 1.
§ See, among other passages, *Ibid.*, i. 22, § 1 ; iii. 6, § 1 ; iii. 8, § 3 ; iv. 6,
§ 7 ; iv. 38, § 8.

Fig. 5. Lamson, p. 103.

from the fact, that, in the passage above quoted, the very same expressions are applied by him to the human race. "We," says Clement, "existed before the foundation of the world, existing first in God himself, inasmuch as we were destined to exist."

The Fathers ascribed to the Son a sort of metaphysical or potential existence in the Father; that is, they supposed that he existed in him from all eternity as an attribute, — his *logos*, reason, or wisdom; that, before the formation of the world, this attribute acquired by a voluntary act of the Father a distinct personal subsistence, and became his instrument in the creation. The germ of this doctrine will be found in the passage above given.

That the Logos was originally regarded by Clement, in common with the other Fathers, as the reason or wisdom of God, is undoubted. Like other attributes or qualities, it was sometimes represented figuratively as speaking and acting. By a transition not very difficult in an age accustomed to speculations of the subtilest nature, if intelligible at all, it came at length to be viewed as a real being or person, having a distinct personal subsistence. Still the former modes of expression were not for a long time wholly laid aside. Traces of the old doctrine are visible among the Fathers of Clement's time. Clement himself sometimes speaks of the Logos as an attribute. He calls the Son expressly "a certain energy or operation of the Father." * And, again, he speaks of the Logos of the Father of the universe as "the wisdom and goodness of God most manifest," or most fully manifested.†

None of the Platonizing Fathers before Origen have acknowledged the inferiority of the Son in more explicit terms than Clement. Photius, writing in the ninth century, besides charging him, as already said, with making the Son a "creature" (*Cod.* 109), says that he used other "impious words full of blasphemy," in a work which has since perished. Rufinus, too, accuses him of calling the "Son of God a creature." ‡

We might quote numerous passages from Clement in which

---

* *Stromata*, lib. vii. c. 2, p. 833, ed. Potter.

† *Stromata*, lib. v. c. 1, p. 646.   ‡ Jerome, *Apol. adv. Rufin.*, lib. ii.

Fig. 6. Lamson, p. 124.

Selected Bibliography

The following books are modern translations of the apostolic fathers and other ante-Nicene authors. These works are the primary sources for the quotations contained in this book.

Eusebius Pamphilus. *Ecclesiastical History*. Translated by Christian Frederick Cruse. 1850. Reprint. Grand Rapids: Baker, 1955.

Jurgens, W. A., ed. *The Faith of the Early Fathers*. 2 vols. Collegeville, Minn.: Liturgical Press, 1979.

Lightfoot, J. B., and J. R. Harmer, eds. *The Apostolic Fathers*. 1891. Reprint. Grand Rapids: Baker, 1984.

Richardson, Cyril C., ed. *Early Christian Fathers*. The Library of Christian Classics, vol. 1. New York: Collier Books, 1970.

Index of Proper Names